TALLAHASSEE COMMUNITY COLLEGE LIBRARY

3 5801 11443948 2

Y0-CMN-319

WITHDRAWN FROM TSC LIBRARY

FLA
F
316
.2
.B3

Barnebey, Faith
Integrity is the issue

DATE DUE			
FEB 1			
MAY 2			
OCT 2 6			

Integrity Is the Issue

FAITH HIGH BARNEBEY

INTEGRITY
IS THE ISSUE
Campaign Life with Robert King High

E. A. SEEMANN PUBLISHING, INC.
Miami, Florida

Copyright © 1971 by Faith High Barnebey

Library of Congress Catalog Card No.: 78-188916

ISBN 0-912458-05-4

All rights reserved including rights of reproduction and use in any form or by any means, including the making of copies by any photo process, or by any electronic or mechanical device, printed or written or oral, or recording for sound or visual reproduction or for use in any knowledge or retrieval system or device, unless permission in writing is obtained from the copyright proprietors.

Manufactured in the United States of America

To Bobby, Holly, Cindy, Valerie, Bonnie Lou, and Susie

"I have fought the good fight, I have finished the race, I have kept the faith."
II Timothy 4:7

Contents

Illustrations 9
Acknowledgments 11
Prologue 13
1. The man 18
2. The High Road 27
3. The Beginning 38
4. The Decision 47
5. "Hey, Look Me Over!" 54
6. The Campaign 66
7. Under the Sun 83
8. Laugh Your Way Through Hell 99
9. A Real Cliff-Hanger 115
10. The Big Push 128
11. Run With the Wind 139
12. The Magic City Explodes 151
13. Summer Song 162
14. A Camp Divided 181
15. Then, in a Moment 191
16. The Dream 198
17. The Dream That Would Not Die 212
Epilogue 220

Illustrations

Mayor Robert King High   30
Mayor High in Havana   36
With President Kennedy   40
Dade County Headquarters, gubernatorial race of 1964   55
Election night, gubernatorial race of 1964   60
With Vice President Johnson at Miami's Torch of Friendship   67
Campaigning in rural Florida   75
Campaigning with Daddy High   75
Mayor High's Father   80
In the voting booth   114
Mayor High in his campaign headquarters   121
Election morning, 1966   135
Father and son campaigning, 1966   160
Mayor High   168

Acknowledgments

For the many friends, members of the press corps, and campaigners who contributed to this book, I am deeply grateful. However, three must be singled out for special mention:

my Creator. That His direction was tangible I have not the slightest doubt;

my friend Bella Kelly of the *Miami News,* who offered sound professional advice and who introduced me to

Fred Shaw of Miami-Dade Junior College and the *Miami Herald,* teacher, philosopher, critic. "Slow down!'" he said a thousand times, remarkable for his patience with impatience.

With such help this book should be perfect. It's not, of course. And for its imperfections, the author takes full credit.

F. B.

Prologue

This is a true story.

No names have been changed to protect the innocent, for those of us who participated in the action were not innocents. Involved, because we chose to be. Naive, perhaps. Helpless, at times. But unwilling participants, never.

When I first considered telling this story, I cannot say. The thought was more like a hidden awareness, given a kick every now and then by some violent human emotion or a dramatic event.

The first stirring may have come when President Kennedy told Bob his idea wasn't so far-fetched, as a matter of fact he thought it a great one; or, that muggy day on the steps of the Pensacola courthouse when Bob faced a hostile crowd, waiting for a bullet. Sounds melodramatic? It was in a way, for only truth has such melodrama.

In analyzing the truth, I tried to take a lesson from my reporter friends, to be as objective as is humanly possible, to state the facts as I lived them, as I witnessed them, and as they were told to me by others. The facts must speak for themselves; most of them are a matter of public record. But public record omits the human element--what the senses perceive, how the emotions react, what motivates the passions of man. Much of the knowledge I was privy to is in direct narrative, but occasionally the story tells itself. It had to.

Truth, as it revealed itself to me, is the moving force behind this book. The people, the events, the human motives that conspired to make a story, are set forth in the hope that man might better understand himself and in understanding, dare to achieve his own Eldorado.

That was how it was with Bob High.

It was a typically warm, humid night in early November--typically, because this was Miami, the Magic City of Florida's Gold Coast. The moon, made famous in story and song, cut a brilliant swath across Bayshore Drive; a white-pillared home, set far back from the street and glowing through the inkiness of oaks and mango trees, threw some of that brilliance back at the sky.

Something was happening at the house on the bluff. Every window, upstairs and down, blazed with light; the long driveway and even part of the lawn were filled with cars, many of them bearing the call letters of radio and television stations. Yet it was obvious no calamity brought those cars. There was something else, something jubilant, a party atmosphere that spilled all the way down to the street.

Inside, the first floor rooms were filled with men screwing flash bulbs into cameras, juggling coffee cups and note pads, sipping and scribbling as they poked through doorways; others moved restlessly around the pool table, lining up a shot, or cringed at each slap of the spinning balls, as they paced nervously around the room. The cigarette smoke and guffaws suggested relaxation, but a current of tension ran through the men as they waited. And it was obvious they were waiting, just killing time.

Upstairs, the noise of a TV filtered through closed bedroom doors. "The polls in Miami have been closed only a short while," an announcer's voice said, "but we do have a few early returns from elsewhere in the state. From Tampa, on the hotly-contested Governor's seat, Miami Mayor Robert King High leads--"

"He's winning! He's winning! " Childish shrieks drowned out the rest of the newscaster's words.

"Yea-a-a! "

"You're ahead, Daddy! "

"Sh-h-h! Not so loud," I cautioned the group of children tumbled among pillows in front of the television. But their excitement was contagious, and I laughed with them.

I looked into my husband's eyes, beyond the sparkle, and won-

Prologue 15

dered, how does it really feel? Those intent blue eyes looking back at me—eyes which some of our friends teasingly called baby blue—belonged to the 1966 Democratic nominee for Governor of Florida, Robert King High, who also happened to be my husband. Had I not been his wife for almost thirteen years, his eyes would have been difficult, if not impossible, to read; but underneath his nonchalent stare were all the proper emotions. Excitement. Anticipation. Urgency.

"Take the High Road" was his first campaign slogan when he ran for Mayor of Miami nine years before. And what a long road it had been to this present night when a young man from Tennessee hoped to become Governor of his adopted state.

"Think it means anything? " I asked, referring to the newscast.

"No, no—not yet, Honey." But there was happiness in his voice, and a bit of awe that the dream might really come true.

Five of our six children—Susan Jill was only two and already in bed—caught the excitement Bob's voice had tried to cover, and their renewed giggles and grins drew him into a pillow fight. In the turmoil of a political campaign, our children could make him forget the strict and often grim realities of the game.

Our son looked disdainfully at his giggly sisters and marched from the room, transistor radio stuck to the side of his head. His daddy followed, dashing downstairs to confer with aides. Bob never walked when he could run.

The votes continued to trickle in, see-sawing back and forth, and my emotions did the same thing. Unendurable excitement finally gave way to numbness as I dressed and combed, blissfully unaware of escaping minutes.

Bob rushed back through the door, bristling with energy and impatience. "Faith, come on! Let's go! " But he was smiling.

All five feet six inches of him was wound up tight, yet he looked handsome in conservative navy blue, striped tie, and, since television likes light blue better than white, a light blue shirt. The papers called his hair red, but one thing about my complex husband the camera could not capture was his mobility, his quality of being vital.

Those waves of vitality began a slow roll in my direction, caught me up, and I came to life once more. Ready at last and glancing around the room to be sure I wasn't forgetting anything, I became aware of a strange sensation.

Our bedroom with its heavy blue draperies, quiet carpeting of the same color, muted wallpaper, was a peaceful retreat, but tonight it almost seemed the inanimate was trying to tell me something. Good grief, I must be going out of my mind! I closed the door, shutting in those fancies, and went down to join Bob.

It had begun. Our family room seemed more like a TV studio with cords snaking across the brick floor, panelled walls glaring under high-powered lights. The cameras were clicking on an all-too-familiar scene.

"Mr. Mayor, how does it feel to know that in a few hours you'll be Governor?"

"Do you have a prediction on the number of votes?"

"Will you look this way one more time, MR. GOVERNOR!"

Bob laughed delightedly at his sudden elevation in title. More significantly, the other faces crinkled into grins and reporters sprinkled the room with cheers; these men had traveled all over the state with Bob, covering the campaign at its best and its worst; they had been around, knew politics and people inside out. Cynical, they were called. And they had broken into a spontaneous burst of emotion.

There was a reason, deeper than surface excitement, and a flicker of susceptibility crossed Bob's face, though he tried not to show it. During the long months of campaigning, reporters and candidate had developed something among them, and for a second they allowed it to escape for me to see. But I was too close. Later I would understand.

Time to leave, Bob said, and another scramble of confusion followed as lights were unplugged, papers gathered up, cigarettes stubbed out, and coffee gulped down. We had already told our other children goodnight, and now Bonnie Lou reached up shyly for a kiss.

"I love you, Daddy." The little head, blond curls still damp from a bath, bent down, and she smiled at a spot on the floor.

Bob was holding my hand, pulling me toward the back door, and I hesitated, turning to look into the kitchen. There came a piercing stab of unfamiliarity about the scene; even though I knew

Prologue 17

by rote the blue-and-white room with its harvest table, it was as if I were suddenly seeing it for the first time. I was in the room yet standing off somewhere to the side, viewing the scene and the Unknown. That was it, that was what the bedroom upstairs had been trying to whisper. The Unknown. What destiny lay ahead, what changes would have occurred in our lives by the time we returned to this room? There was a sense of change and the inevitable, and from Bob's expression, I knew he felt it, too. For a moment, though surrounded by people, we were completely alone.

The slamming of car doors sounded like a quick succession of firecrackers on the Fourth of July, and the caravan was off. Within minutes the car was careening toward the bright lights of the city's center and the Everglades Hotel, where we would wait with supporters for the returns. Our heads bent close to the radio, listening intently. There was no conversation, scarcely a breath. Too much was at stake.

Palm-lined Biscayne Boulevard was jammed with cars. Many of those cars wore "High for Governor" signs, and as their occupants recognized Bob, horns blared, arms flashed out of windows in greeting. "Good luck, Mr. Mayor! " and "We're with you! " voices shouted.

A crowd was gathered at the hotel entrance, and their expressions of welcome turned to surprise when we pulled down a ramp leading underneath the hotel. This procedure was a part of elaborate security measures, made necessary by shocking events in recent weeks. There was also a man quietly stationed among the trees at our home; he would watch and wait throughout the long night.

Ernie Bush was waiting for us in the parking tunnel. A friend and a detective with the Department, he was responsible for security tonight. As we followed him through a maze of grey concrete passageways to a service elevator, my imagination ran riot with the cloak-and-dagger atmosphere. It would have been a ball, but I could never forget that events right out of a TV drama made this necessary. As we stepped into the elevator, I looked at Bob's face. His mind was a million miles away.

He was thinking of the future, the now, and the many circumstances that had led to this slow ride up.

# CHAPTER ONE

The Man

All men have a philosophical premise; events and circumstances influence their every thought and action. Bob High's premise was tied up in three words: The Great Depression. Born in Flat Creek, Tennessee, April 9, 1924, he was thrust into a world suddenly grown adult. Money and the security it bought vanished overnight, and in its place came hunger. Many families in rural America gave up their farms and moved to the city to survive. The Highs were such a family.

Lester High, a carpenter-farmer by trade, took his wife, two daughters, son, and everything he could pile into a wagon, to Chattanooga. Bob, or Robert, as his parents called him, was the baby of the family in years only. When he was five, he sold the newspaper which earned him the nickname "Grit": the paper's motto, "A quitter never wins, and a winner never quits," impressed him, and five years later he bought a lawn mower on his own credit; to pay it off he mowed lawns, delivered groceries and milk.

Years later he recalled, "The only nice part of the dairy job was that I could drink all the milk I wanted! " He never forgot having to get up at four in the morning and go out in the hurting cold; years later the memory would draw him to the sunshine and warmth of Florida. But right now the fine-edge honing of the boy, the man, had begun.

Though lacking in material necessities, the High family had in abundance a deep faith in God. Daddy High always reminded listeners, "Robert learned the Bible at his mother's knee," and with a chuckle and twist of his sharp-boned face, "I guess it did him some good! "

For some the Depression years brought despair, a rut with no future; for young Robert it triggered determination. With grown-up responsibilities came the knowledge of what it meant to earn his way, and with these same responsibilities came the beginning of ambition. Someday he would have fine clothes. Someday he would be someone. He played a game with himself sometimes, pretending he was "a senator or something" in Washington, writing down comments on affairs of state in a little, black dog-eared notebook. A childish game, Daddy High thought, and he'd smile.

Teen-aged Bob's determination grew. It protected him when he had to serve his high school contemporaries at the soda fountain and pretend that he too could dawdle on streetcorners and jingle a pocketful of coins; it was alive, though breathing heavily, when he attended the Senior Prom in an R.O.T.C. uniform, ignoring the whispers because he was not dressed in evening clothes like the other boys. He turned this disadvantage around and organized a four-piece band, "The Sophisticates" in R.O.T.C. uniforms—until the boys could afford tuxedos!

It was a short hop from bandleader to high school graduate, and fifteen-year-old Bob decided he was ready to make his appearance on the world scene. Since opportunities in Chattanooga were dim, he decided to run away.

Lured by the prospect of Big Jobs in Nashville, he and a buddy quietly left their sleeping houses and hitchhiked to that city. They arrived with seven cents, and a newspaper with its want ads cost a nickel. By nightfall they had two cents, no job, no food, and nowhere to sleep. There was one way out.

"I guess we can spend the night at my grandma's," Bob sighed.

One night stretched into several, no jobs materialized, and on the fourth morning two dejected youths headed back to the highway. They were going home.

Daddy High walked slowly toward home. He had been to the market where Bob worked; for the past three days it seemed as if he and his wife, Kate, had done nothing else but look for their son. They didn't have a telephone, so it was a slow business, calling on relatives, then friends. "Have you seen Robert?" The answer was always no. He was worried, and he mulled over the advice given by his son's former employer. "When he does turn up, don't be too hard on him!"

He was so deep inside himself—as a matter of fact, he was praying—that he nearly missed the tableau through the porch window: the prodigal son, seated, facing his mother. It was obvious Kate was doing all the talking, and Daddy High paused. What would he say to the boy? The prodigal son, he pondered, the story from the Bible. All at once, he knew.

"Well." Daddy High looked his son in the eye, clapped a hand down hard on his shoulder. "I hope you enjoyed your trip."

That was all. His son's face told him it was enough.

Bob stayed home and went to vocational school, became a welder, then went to New Orleans for work in a shipyard. With the advent of World War II, however, the shipyard's production changed, so he found a job in a women's shoe store, part of a national chain. He did well, and the company promoted him to assistant manager of their Baton Rouge store. It was a good job, but somehow, something was missing; these were not the challenges the boy from Tennessee had dreamed about.

Baton Rouge was a college town. The youthful assistant manager envied the students who came in the store; they had assurance, the polish of education. He took to walking by the campus on afternoons off, and finally the great state university cast its spell. He called home and told his parents he was coming back to go to college.

The men at the store gave him a going-away party, and the manager, who had become a sort of elder brother, gave him a five-year diary. There was a note on the last page:

"Wonder where and what you and I will be when you make this final entry (December 31, 1947). Till then, may you achieve the same results in your endless quest for knowledge as you have in your pursuit of 'stuff and things.' Lots of luck."

"Keep the diary up, Bob," his friend said. "Someday you'll be glad you did."

The Man

Bob's first entry was made the next day. "On my way home in my new car—a '37 De Soto that won't run at all or runs like hell!"

His studies at the University of Chattanooga were short-lived; he took a dim view of going to school with a war on, so he enlisted in the Army Air Corps. Army life, too, ended abruptly, for during basic training he received a serious back injury, and in a delicate spinal operation, a steel plate was fused in his back.

The restless patient spent nearly a year in Army hospitals. To occupy his mind he wrote in his diary ("They keep you as clean here on the inside as out!") and devoured books. His reading gave clue to the stirrings within: *The Life of Andrew Jackson, The Civil War, Inside Europe, Inside Latin America,* and Churchill's *Blood, Sweat and Tears.* He followed the progress of the war closely, made random notes. "Mopping up in Tunis". . . "France was invaded at 3:02 this morning (June 26, 1943)." He wondered at the psychology of a Hitler, didn't understand it, so he added another subject to his studies. Most of all, he did a lot of thinking.

Bob the patient was nearly ready to become Bob the Veteran; he knew he had a job waiting for him in Chattanooga, at a shoe store. And yet. There was still a college education to reckon with, and an insistent gnawing told him Chattanooga was not the place for it.

He was in an Army hospital in Jacksonville, Florida, and his bed was next to the window. He could look out and see the sunshine, the palm trees, the tropics. He liked what he saw.

It was June of 1944, a sweltering early-summer day in Miami, Florida. Bob stepped off the train, grinning at the blast of heat. This was the Magic City, the tropics, and a case of love at first sight. Back injury healed, he walked briskly out of the depot into the beginning of a new life.

The yearnings from childhood to manhood had finally matured, and after discharge from the hospital and a few weeks at home, he made his decision to finish college in the sun. He enrolled at the University of Miami under the GI Bill and sold used cars on the side. Later he transferred to the Law School of Stetson University in Deland; he supplemented his income there by working as a hospital orderly on the midnight shift.

It was a struggle working all night and keeping up with studies by day, but the law degree was finally his. The idea of becoming an attorney had developed over the years, from a little boy who listened with fascination to the courtroom tales of a favorite relative to the young man who adopted Thomas Jefferson as his ideal. He wanted to pattern his own life after the great statesman—and Jefferson had begun as a lawyer. Aptitude tests in the Air Force strengthened this resolve. Their results: the fields of law and political science.

The beginning of Robert King High's career as an attorney was typical of the man. With mustache (to make him look his twenty-five years), skeleton named Oscar (to use in personal injury cases), and three hundred dollars, he opened offices in the exclusive DuPont Building in downtown Miami.

Why the DuPont Building? Because it had the prestige a new attorney did not, and because it offered a complete law library. That library was essential; law books were expensive, and Bob had spent his entire capital on a second-hand desk and a month's rent. It was a first gamble for the man out of law school and would not be the last.

He leaned back in his chair, propped his feet on the desk, and surveyed the magnificent array of empty bookcases. And he waited. A divorce case launched him on his way the first afternoon.

That same divorce case also made him the most embarrassed lawyer in town. The disgruntled husband of the lawsuit, angry because he had to send checks to his ex-wife's attorney, made them out to Robert King High, S.O.B. And every month the red-faced lawyer endorsed them: Robert King High, S.O.B.

Since Miami was his adopted home, Bob needed permanent roots; as a practicing attorney, he wanted the appearance of stability that, to him, could be provided by only one thing: a home. To decide was to act, so he bought a house. Fifty dollars and the GI Bill got him three bedrooms (he painted his chocolate brown), a cypress-panelled living room and dining room, a galley-type kitchen; it all backed up to a huge, man-made lake. He invited a close friend in the insurance business to share the home and expenses with him, so bachelors Bob and Bill Poorbaugh (Poorboy, to his friends) set up housekeeping and stability.

The Man

Poorboy, crew-cut, well-scrubbed, eager, had a ruling passion. He would figure the odds on anything. During the war his plane was badly shot up, and the pilot asked the crew if they wanted to stay with the plane or bail out and take their chances. Over the radio came Navigator Bill's, "Hold it a minute, Sir!" With shells exploding all around, he scribbled frantically, covering the paper with percentage points. In a moment his exultant voice came back over the radio. "The odds are with us, Sir! I'm stickin' with the plane!"

Poorboy prided himself on his accuracy. One afternoon, while making preparations for a threatening hurricane, Bob suggested that Bill put his new automobile under the carport. Bill scoffed. He figured the odds were his car would be just as safe in the driveway. The storm arrived, and Bill stood at the window, watching debris fly by. He suddenly yelled.

"Hey, Bob! C'mere quick!" He laughed nervously. "Look at that car, Bob. Just look at my new car! Heh-heh-heh!"

The next-door neighbor's tree had fallen across Bill's car, flattening the center and making pillow puffs out of the front and rear ends. Bill stared. "Guess I figured wrong."

Bob shook his head, chuckling. Neither realized they would someday rely heavily on Bill's passion for figuring the odds.

Between law cases (which were coming steadily now), Bob worked at playing. The depression years had left their mark; play was a stranger and he set about making friends with it, at first cautiously, then with abandon, as if he had a premonition of the years ahead. He bought a blue Cadillac and had a telephone installed in it; he filled his closet with suits, shirts, ties—things the boy vowed he would have someday; he bought a boat, a runabout, and like a child at Christmastime tore back and forth across the lake. He developed a keen love for the water, and defying the steel plate in his back, learned to water ski. He enjoyed the novelty of play but didn't give himself entirely to it, even for the moment; his mind and body were too accustomed to a pattern of drive.

He did give himself to people, especially children. Neighborhood youngsters trailed him like the Pied Piper, and he was never too busy to take them for a spin around the lake or pile them into his car and let them talk to their parents on the car phone. Neighbors noticed the obvious. Bachelor Bob loved children and children loved him.

"Isn't it a shame he doesn't have a family of his own? " they whispered.

Bob was a step ahead of them. His reactions, like his working pace, were fast, and love was no exception. He was lunching with a municipal judge one rainy day, letting his eyes roam aimlessly around the room; his eyes suddenly stopped and focused on a booth directly across from them.

"What is it? " the Judge asked.

"See that girl over there? "

The Judge looked. He saw a petite girl, around nineteen, with auburn-colored hair that was very wet. She was munching on a hamburger, obviously a refugee from the streaming rain. "Yes, I see her."

Bob rubbed a finger across his upper lip (the mustache has been cast into oblivion) and smiled. "That's the girl I'm going to marry! "

The Judge looked startled. "Who is she? "

"I don't know," he answered quietly. "But I'm going to find out."

And he did. His romance was true to the man, for it progressed with the speed of a hurricane. He met the girl in October, and on March 27, 1954, he married her.

The girl was me.

Bill Poorbaugh moved out of the house and I moved in. There were times in our early months of marriage when I wondered if Poorboy wasn't better equipped to manage a home than I. Bob smiled through charred steaks, rocky biscuits (I couldn't even make the canned ones turn out right), and unperked coffee, gallantly complimenting me on all' three.

Our marriage was probably saved the day he learned he was to become a father. I bought a pair of blue booties by way of telling him, carefully wrapped them, and was on my way to pick him up at the office. The DuPont Building loomed ahead. Bob was standing on the curb, waved, and came around to the driver's side, as I slid over and handed him the package.

The streets were jammed with five o'clock traffic and people were pouring from nearby offices. We came to a stop light. Bob tore into the package, looked up and shouted a strangled laugh, and began yelling to the policeman on the corner—blue booties dangling out the window! Passers-by stared at the madman, took in the booties, then cheered and clapped while I burrowed under the floor.

Bob's jubilation of that day was exceeded only by his performance when little Bobby arrived. His emotions went from exploding joy ("Faith, you gave me a BOY!") to a deep and humble gratitude that God gave him a healthy child. To Bob, a family was the highest expression of love, a tangible security the world could not touch. This security became even greater when, fifteen months later, red-haired Holly was born. He was meant to be a father. Now that he had two children of his own to add to the neighborhood's growing collection, he assumed a new-found solidity; his attitude said, I am a family man.

The new role did not diminish his humor, however; it ran to the tongue-in-cheek, and friends were never quite certain when he was serious or when he was kidding. Bob had a favorite device we came to call "The Patsy," for in me, he had the perfect victim.

One Sunday morning our church had a visiting pastor, and as we were leaving, I saw him standing in a corner, alone. "Look, Bob," I whispered. "Isn't that the minister who gave the sermon? Everyone is passing him by! Let's go over for a second."

"What?" Bob looked blank.

"I said, the poor man is practically being ignored! He gave a good sermon. The least we can do is tell him!"

A funny expression crossed Bob's face. "Isn't that a shame," he said. "You're right! You go right ahead."

I wondered why Bob hung back but assumed he would follow me. "Good morning." I smiled at the dignified-looking gentleman. "We certainly enjoyed your sermon."

The man stooped down a trifle, peered at me through his spectacles, and said, "H-How's that?"

"I said, we enjoyed your sermon this morning. Your sermon." My poise was dwindling. The man looked at me strangely.

At this point good old Bob rambled up. "Why, Honey, you've

made a mistake. This gentleman isn't our visiting minister. He's over there," and he pointed across the foyer where a large crowd was gathered around a distinguished looking, bespectacled man. The Patsy had played into his hands!

The practical jokes went on, Bob's law practice grew steadily, and he devoted more time to community affairs, eventually managing the campaign for an unsuccessful city commission candidate. Though his small taste of politics was fruitless (he had also lost a Justice of the Peace race while a bachelor), his appetite was whetted. And as a dejected campaign manager for a losing candidate, he would not have believed his own appointment with destiny was around the corner.

CHAPTER TWO

The High Road

Bob thought over the events of the day with disbelief. He checked his watch—not really caring what time it was, it was just a habit—and wondered at the change a few hours had brought in his life.

It began as an ordinary day in late summer, 1957, when Bob received a call from an attorney friend asking him to come to his office and meet someone. The "someone" was former Miami Mayor Abe Aronovitz, retired from public office and highly respected in the city.

The present city leadership was taking the wrong direction, Mayor Aronovitz said, and he cared about his city. Politicians were filling the needs of politics rather than the people, and he couldn't sit back and watch it happen. He was involving himself again, he said, looking for a young man to run for Mayor against the machine in the coming November race.

Mr. Abe, as some affectionately called him, was the elder statesman of Miami with no axe to grind. While Mayor, he had stepped on toes and made enemies, but he left office with an unquestioned honesty and reputation. He was looking for those same qualities, someone who would be a fighter, and he reached the conclusion that Bob High was the man.

Mayor Aronovitz offered his support and public endorsement, a consideration not to be taken lightly. As Bob mulled over their conversation, he tried to pretend a carefully weighed decision, but he knew instinctively what the answer would be. The decision was made a long time ago, when a little farm boy kicked at the dusty roads of Tennessee.

Big Miami was accustomed to taking its politics in stride, but a five foot six inch political unknown was about to hand the Magic City a campaign as it had never seen.
At campaign time the city's politicians played the role of the last of the big-time spenders, waging a war of billboards and TV. At the outset Bob established Rule No. 1: no campaign contributions over $250 would be accepted (and there were few of these!). He told the voters that big money meant big favors in return, and the office of Mayor wasn't for sale at any price. The lack of well-padded financing distinguished his campaign from the beginning. It proved an advantage.
New ideas were born of necessity. Without the expensive routes of television and billboards, other methods for getting Bob's name before the voters had to be devised. One late-night session with neighbors yielded an idea which would be copied in years to come. It was football season, and the University of Miami played to huge crowds in the Orange Bowl on Friday nights. Those crowds would see signs carried by volunteers at every entrance to the Orange Bowl: "Take the High Road" and "Robert King High for Mayor."
There remained the problem of getting the signs made, for the campaign could not afford professionally printed posters; so do-it-yourself politics was invented. Young mothers, after their children were bedded down for the night, doubled over poster boards, ran through jars and jars of paint, squinted critically at the results; their husbands put the signs together under the expert direction of Daddy High, who had journeyed down from Tennessee to help his son.
Some who saw the signs at the Orange Bowl thought they advertised a high school--Robert King High--but the hours of painting and hammering paid off. Newspapers and TV picked up the story, and the harvest of publicity drew people to Bob at succeeding football games; they wanted to shake hands with this newcomer who flaunted political tradition.
Mayor Aronovitz campaigned actively, and crowds enjoyed his definition of an honest man: "You lock him in a room for twenty-

The High Road

four hours with a million one-dollar bills. If the million is still there when you let him out, you've an honest man who knows just how much money a million dollars really is!" The salt-and-pepper-haired gentleman with his pointed parables was no fly-by-night and the voters knew it. They listened.

Though short on financing, political pros, and organizational genius, the campaign attracted an enthusiastic, if not fanatical, following. Amateurs all, with the exception of Mayor Aronovitz, they believed; perhaps that was the key. The candidate and his followers would soon know if that belief was contagious, for election day arrived.

When the votes were counted, out of a field of five candidates, the incumbent Mayor had 10,514, and his closest opponent, Bob High, had 8,264. In Miami elections fifty per cent plus one means a winner, so the two were thrown into a run-off.

Two weeks later it was all over. A startled Miami found itself with a new Mayor, thirty-three year old Robert King High. He had promised them nothing except honest government. Evidently that was what the voters wanted.

There was a bit of unfinished business, and on the Friday night after the election football fans were greeted at the Orange Bowl with signs which read, "Thank you, Miami--Robert King High." If people had been surprised before, they were dumbfounded now. Whoever heard of remembering the voters after an election! But as Bob said during the campaign, politics as usual was on the way out. His statement set the tone for the years ahead.

Bob's first term in office was bitter. Old-line politicians resented the "young upstart" with his insistence that government should benefit the people and ridiculed him at every opportunity. One reporter wrote that some of the commission sessions could be classified as gang rumbles if the participants were juveniles instead of elected representatives of the people.

More than once he was invited to join "the other side." One day, on an out of town trip for the city with another official, an offer was made.

"Look, Bob, you can't fight it." The official leaned close, lowered his voice. "Why don't you come in with us?"

"How do you mean?" Bob asked, pretending naiveté.

Mayor Robert King High

"We-l-l," the man smiled, "There's big money floating around. You're a young man, and—nobody'd ever know."

Bob shook his head.

The official shrugged. "If you ever change your mind, just remember, the door is always open." Then he paused. "But if you ever say anything about this to anyone, I'll call you a damn liar to your face."

The battle lines were drawn. Bob remembered Mr. Abe's words, "a fighter." They would get a fight, all right.

The next day at City Hall, an influential visitor from the north angrily paced Bob's office. "I just want you to know, Mr. Mayor, that I will never set foot in this city again! "

The previous night Bob's visitor had gone to a downtown club. He did not know it had deteriorated from a supper club to a clip joint, until he and his business associate, after a short stay, were handed a bill for four hundred dollars. He protested, and the grinning owner offered to let the police settle the dispute. It was a case of simple blackmail, because the owner knew his customer could not afford the resulting publicity from his arrest in such a place.

Bob was upset. He knew a wide-open town was a self-defeating town; the visitor who was gypped did not come back; the family man looking for a decent place to raise his family went elsewhere. And he knew the conditions which made a wide-open town possible could not exist without the protection of politicians and law enforcement officials. Something had to be done, and he believed the Mayor was the one to do it.

As Mayor, he was only one vote out of five, and the way things were going at the city commission meetings, he was lucky to end up on the losing side of a 3-2 vote. Because he was a loner, he had to use unorthodox methods; and because he was a politician, he knew what the crooked official feared most: public attention. He used it as a weapon.

With a newsman by his side, he toured Miami's strip joints. The expedition was good for a running series on how the customer was fleeced—B-girls, booze, and official corruption that must exist for the tourist trap to stay in business. Bob kept the issue alive through TV and headlines, and eventually clip-joint row began to tumble.

Bolita, the numbers racket, was his next target. To prove his contention that the game was running without interference, he dressed in old clothes and a battered cap and went on a buying tour. It was no accident that a reporter went with him.

The next day Miamians saw a familiar face splashed across the front page: their Mayor, holding bolita ticket number thirty-three. Aroused citizens applied pressure, even phoning in tips to Bob because they "knew he'd investigate!" One call came the day after the bolita incident.

"Mayor High?" The man was indignant. "I've got something for you to check out!"

"Yes, sir. What is it?"

"Right across the street from me, every night for the past week, two policemen spend a couple of hours inside this house. There's something fishy going on!"

Bob promised to look into the matter, and that night with another official, drove to the address. Sure enough, there was the police car but no criminal activities. Two young policemen, rookies, were visiting their girl friends.

When Bob tapped on the door, one of the startled rookies blinked his eyes. "My God! You never know where you'll see him!"

In time the racketeers and manipulators grew aggressive. Bob received threatening calls daily, information that a "contract" was out for him. He kept pushing.

The voters approved his methods, for in November of '59 they returned the "fiery little redhead," as newsmen dubbed him, to office.

He gained national attention as a crusader, and later *Life Magazine* selected him as one of a hundred outstanding young Americans. When the *Life* issue carrying the feature hit the newsstands, he brought one home. He sat down, stared at it a long, long time.

"Can you imagine that?" he asked quietly.

Slowly and persistently the sacred cows began to topple. The job was no easier, but by now it was palatable; the "old" commission members had been retired by the ballot, and meetings were no longer name-calling hassles. A new city commission rolled up its sleeves.

City insurance business was ludicrous. Patronage practices allowed each of the five commissioners to award one-fifth of the business to cronies. "Packages" were equally divided until finally, two or three buildings were left. The result? The north half of a building might be insured by one company, the south half by another! A long overdue competitive bid system was installed.

Bob went statewide, successfully leading campaigns to force Florida Power and Light to cut consumer rates; the City intitated a study of Southern Bell, with the result that the Public Service Commission ordered major reductions in phone rates. The studies showed that both utility companies, in the space of four years, had overcharged their customers by $225,000,000.

One writer called Bob "a modern day David" because of his battles with the giants of business; and the giants kept coming. An automobile insurance rate hike was requested. The City of Miami rushed auditors to Tallahassee to analyze data and request a delay, and the City's legal staff, at the Commission's direction, intervened as the public's advocate. Hearings were held in affected areas and the rate hike rejected.

There was one more Goliath, the largest of all: Florida East Coast Railway. Again the City of Miami intervened. The FEC dispute went all the way to Washington, and when it was finally resolved, the powerful DuPont interests were forced to pay two years' back taxes on the FEC, and a total of 1.9 million dollars to cities up and down the east coast of Florida.

Bob's working days stretched into eighteen hours, yet he still had a law practice to maintain. Even fellow commissioners urged him to slow down.

"Don't have time! " he quipped. "Besides, if public officials don't care about the people who elect them—the little guys—who will? "

Fatigue lines around his eyes deepened alarmingly.

Bob found his days and weeks filled with more than crime and law and local problems. As chance had it, he was a natural to lead in an area peculiar to the City of Miami, an area dealing with matters South American. Because of its geographic location, Miami was the logical "Gateway to the Americas," but it was occasionally nosed into second place by New Orleans. As Mayor, he was determined to make Miami number one and keep it there.

He started with an advantage. He spoke the language. While still a law student, he had attended the University of Havana for a summer session to learn Spanish; he had a feeling it would be a handy thing for a young lawyer to know, especially in Miami. In Havana he lived in a Cuban home, so if he wanted to eat, he had to learn the language. He learned.

Now, with the prospect of keeping the Gateway to the Americas open and inviting, he realized how important that long-ago summer session was.

Miami and its economy are synonymous with the word tourist, not only from the icy north, but from South America. Since nothing can supplant first-hand knowledge, Bob led goodwill trips to the south, encouraging an exchange of cultures, selling Miami—and he sold it in their own language. The response surpassed imagination.

Titles are held in high esteem south of the border, and here was someone with a title, with whom they could communicate. Bob found his neighbors to the south as responsive as Miami supporters. He was called upon to inaugurate new air routes, inspect bridges and roads; he spoke before cheering senators in Ecuador and visited slums in Peru, where the natives carried him on their shoulders and named a street after him. In unspoken exchanges he was able to let them know he cared and many times he ended a speech with the words, *somos hermanos.* We are brothers.

Bob collected many memories, many momentos. Once, at the conclusion of a successful tour in Mexico City, he said goodbye to *Los Charros,* the distinguished gentlemen cowboys of Mexico. They were often together during his stay and now presented him with a gold-embroidered sombrero, a group gift. Suddenly one of the younger charros, a chunky, serious-faced youth, stepped forward.

"I want give you something, from me." He spoke haltingly, his face red. "I am sorry I have not better gift. Please."

He stooped down, quickly unbuckled his spurs. They were sterling silver, used only for parades, and a prized possession. He handed them to Bob. "You take, please."

Somos hermanos.

Bob developed an unusual relationship with some of the Latin governments. Heads of state, ignoring the protocol of dealing only with officials of equal rank, invited him to their countries; a few returned his visits. One trip south provided him with the springboard for a story he never tired of telling.

He was dining with the President of a Central American country. The President grew warm, removed his jacket, and without a backward glance, flung it carelessly over his shoulder. Immediately a bodyguard sprang from nowhere and caught the coat before it touched the floor. Bob was impressed.

In retelling the story, he mentioned how casually the President had flung the jacket aside, how the bodyguard "melted out of the woodwork" to grab it. "So I decided when I got back to Miami, I'd try the same thing.

"I went to the City Commission meeting—," and at this point the audience, remembering the days of anti-High commissioners began to titter, "—and I told my colleagues how warm it was, I thought I'd take my jacket off. So I flung it over my shoulder without a backward glance.

"I just got it back from the cleaners today!"

In addition to the heads of state who returned Bob's visits, dignitaries from all the Central and South American countries were invited to place their country's seal on Miami's Torch of Friendship in Bayfront Park. The Torch, sponsored by an enterprising City Manager, Melvin Reese, and Bob, still burns as a symbol of the ties between the Americas.

Bob gained the reputation as an expert on Latin American affairs; he was decorated by five of these countries, and the papers south of the border called him "The Mayor of the Americas." Washington and the State Department called on him with increasing frequency as a sort of trouble-shooting ambassador of good will. One incident hinted at troubled days ahead.

Batista had been replaced by Fidel Castro, and the State Department, working with the City of Miami, suddenly completed arrangements for a trip to Havana. The purpose of the trip was to re-establish tourism between the United States and Cuba.

The American contingent was met at the airport in Havana by a bearded official. Castro would see them that afternoon, he said,

Mayor High in Havana 1959, waiting to see Fidel Castro

and whisked them to the Capri Hotel. Except for the staff, the mammoth Capri was empty.

Castro cancelled that appointment but set a new one the following day. It was the beginning of a pattern, as cancellation followed cancellation. As a last resort, Bob convinced the group to agree to a meeting at four in the morning, the only hour Fidel could find. Fidel did not appear.

The weary and disgusted Americans stalked out and headed for home. They were hospitably entertained, Bob mused, but they were shown only what the bearded officials, their hosts, wanted them to see. It was almost as if they were under guard. That trip he would write off as a failure, but he could not so easily write off his suspicions.

Nor could he know that Miami and its leadership was about to become the focus of a long-running drama.

CHAPTER THREE

The Beginning

Destiny, the chef with all ingredients, blends place, time, and event, serving them to man. So it was with Bob. The place was Miami, the time was 1960, and the event was the Presidential campaign of John F. Kennedy. The components were presented, swiftly and suddenly.

Robert Kennedy was trying to line up support for his brother, and right now he concentrated on Florida. It was not easy, for few officials in Florida were willing to risk their own fortunes by publicly backing the Senator. They knew Florida politics was ticklish at best. No matter if they espoused similar causes; in the Sunshine State it might be suicidal to back Jack Kennedy. And most of those who lived and died by the vote wanted to stay alive.

Bobby Kennedy talked with Bob High. Bob agreed with RFK that his brother should be the next President, and he wasn't afraid to say so; bucking the pros was nothing new to him. He became the first elected official in Florida to line up publicly with Jack Kennedy. Unwittingly, that act was the first step in his own destiny, for Jack Kennedy would be the catalyst.

Bob took me to meet Senator Kennedy during one of his campaign swings through south Florida. On the way to the airport in West Palm Beach, he spoke of his impressions. "He has vision, a dry wit—obviously he loves the challenge of politics, the art of it." I had to smile. He might have been speaking of himself.

The plane arrived and Bob steered me toward the ramp. "Senator, I want you to meet my wife."

The Beginning 39

"Your wife? " he exclaimed. "I thought she was your daughter! "

"He does have vision," I whispered to Bob.

The New Frontier swept the country. John Kennedy became Bob's President, and in the course of events, his friend. He was sometimes called to Washington to give a run-down on a Florida resident being considered for a particular position. In these matters his research was as methodical as the FBI's: information had to have the validity of legal evidence or it was discarded.

Occasionally the telephone rang late at night, with the President's familiar, clipped, "Bob? " on the other end. Bob's expression always displayed the same mixture of respect, delight, and humility. It seemed to say, "Can you imagine the President of the United States calling *me*? "

The two shared an enthusiasm for Miami's strategic location as the Gateway to the Americas and the importance of inter-country relationships. Shortly after the President's election, Bill Baggs, editor of the *Miami News*, visited the Florida White House in Palm Beach. He was strolling in the garden with Kennedy.

"I like your red-headed Mayor," the President said. "I'd like to appoint him as an ambassador."

"I wish you wouldn't," Baggs drawled. "We need him in Miami! "

Kennedy chuckled. "Well, I may anyway. He's the type of man I want representing this country abroad. Tell me, is he an intellectual? "

"Hell, no! " he laughed. "But he has intelligence and the instinct for what is right."

The President nodded, and they continued their walk.

With the ill-fated Bay of Pigs invasion, liaison between Washington and Miami intensified. Prisoners of the Bay of Pigs, after long and tedious negotiations, were released and flown to Miami.

Bob was among the group of officials and reporters who waited to meet the planes in a guarded area of Miami International Airport. There was a funny tightness in his chest. He'd never had the feeling before, and he assumed excitement put it there. He, Bob High from Flat Creek, was watching history as it happened.

Mayor High greeting President Kennedy in Miami Beach, a few days before the assassination.

The Beginning

He saw hundreds of Cubans on the other side of a heavy chain link fence. They had been waiting for hours, hoping to see a loved one. The planes were late, and anxiety ran through the crowd. He would remember small details later, but right now the drama was upon them. A hum of distant motors, a flash of silver, whirling props reversing to a stop. The sight of haggard but eager faces pressed to the windows, and when the engines were cut, the faint sound of cheers from the belly of the plane. The sight and sounds of democracy, he thought. The doors were opened, steps put in place.

Men, tears streaming down their faces, stepped down the ramp. As the group of officials moved forward, the first prisoner dropped to his knees and kissed the ground of a free America.

Bob followed the buses carrying the men to Dinner Key Auditorium, where they would be reunited with their families. Police motorcycles, sirens screaming, led the way. The sides of the buses were draped with banners proclaiming, "Heroes of the Bay of Pigs!" and all along the route cars screeched to a stop, necks turned, surprised or indignant faces suddenly broke into a grin. Some persons leaped from their cars shouting, "Viva Cuba Libre!" and "Welcome to America!" This was something he'd remember.

Funny. The tightness in his chest was still there. He wished it would go away.

With the eruption of Castro and Communism, thousands upon thousands of Cubans fled to Miami, by air via Mexico or Spain, for those who could afford it, in fishing boats for those who could not. It was exodus in the twentieth century. But the children of Israel spoke Spanish, crossed the Straits of Florida instead of the Red Sea, and came to the land of milk and honey, America.

The sudden influx of nearly 200,000 refugees created chaos. Miami resources were heavily strained, housing was pitifully inadequate, self-supporting jobs were practically non-existent.

There were grumbles of discontent from Miami residents most sorely affected. A housewife finds she has acquired new neighbors overnight: three or maybe four families jammed into a one bedroom box-like structure, children spilling over into her yard. Jobs, once plentiful, are gobbled up, and the Negro population feels the bite; once-wealthy Cubans work as janitors and waiters; women, formerly accustomed to a *finca* with servants, find their positions reversed. It was a trying period, and national attention focused on Miami.

As Mayor, Bob's daily problems were compounded by 200,000. He used the communications media as a mass tranquilizing pill, urging patience, understanding; he made countless trips to Washington, discussing federal aid, resettlement procedures.

The City of Miami attempted to fill in the void for job opportunities. Over weeks of bitter opposition by the taxi-cab companies, the City passed a law making it possible for Cubans to obtain permits to drive a taxi, after road and regulations schooling. Special training courses in various fields sprang up, and once-hesitant employers opened their doors. The people had to eat. It was that simple.

The refugees recognized the problems their arrival created. They wanted desperately to show their love for the American people—Bob in particular. The Mayor of Miami cared. He was their friend, and to these near-homeless peoples, he symbolized all Americans. Word was passed along the Cuban grapevine. "We must find a way! "

The sudden downpour, a common occurrence in Miami, had settled into a fine, misty rain. The black night seemed blacker as headlights were reflected on the wet street.

One set of headlights, thrown quickly to bright by a startled driver, picked out a large group of people moving silently across the street. Some walked in twos and threes; many glanced apprehensively over their shoulders, swift, darting looks. The looks were born of weeks and months of running.

Their destination was a small, shabby building directly ahead, undistinguished from its surroundings, for this was an old section of town where everything was peeling and tired-looking. The people entering the building were tired, too, but they hurried.

They were members of a group which called itself the "Thirtieth of November Revolutionary Movement," a Cuban refugee organization. The room in which they met was dirty, almost bare

The Beginning

of furniture, the type of room that most of these people were unaccustomed to. The few chairs were offered to elderly women. Men leaned against the walls; some took up crouched positions on the floor, carefully, to keep dust off their only suits. There was a table in the center of the room, and it too was dusty. Over it hung a bare light bulb, casting shadows on the assembled faces.

The group was meeting to decide what to do for the Mayor of Miami, their *amigo* . A token, a gesture, something. Ideas were suggested, discarded. No, no, that would be impossible. Impractical. Not good enough. And then, all at once, they found the answer.

"A medal," they said. "A medal for the *alcalde!* "

"Yes, but not just any medal," one responded. "It must be of pure gold." Heads nodded in agreement.

"But we have no money! Where will we get the money? "

There were murmurs, grunts of disgust. It was true. They had crossed the sea with the clothes on their backs, nothing more. A collective sigh went up.

"Gold is expensive. But if we can get the gold," the man's voice was hopeful, "I can contribute something. I will make the most beautiful medal you have ever seen." He was a jeweler, an artisan.

"Just like that, eh? " Their leader's voice was heavy with sarcasm, to hide the despair. "And where will this gold come from? "

There were more whispers. Men shrugged; women looked down, shaking heads. Once it would have been so easy—they could have bought gold as one buys a loaf of bread. Now they couldn't even buy the bread.

"I know a way." The soft voice came from the back of the room. Heads turned, attentive, for it was a voice which carried authority, the quiet kind of assurance that does not need to shout.

The owner of the voice strode forward, and as he came under the light, many recognized him. In Cuba, he had been a successful doctor; now he worked as a busboy. "I know a way," he repeated.

All eyes were on him as he extracted a clean, white handkerchief from his pocket, placed it in the center of the dusty table, and carefully smoothed it out. The faces watched, quizzical. Then he removed his wrist watch. A solid gold one. He looked at it for a moment, gently placed it in the center of the handkerchief, and walked away.

It took less than a minute for the others to absorb what he had done. Then, one by one, they passed in front of the dusty old table. Women removed gold wedding bands, blinking to keep back tears; men twisted and pulled at college rings; an old, old lady unclasped the gold chain from around her neck, kissed the religious figure dangling from it, and tenderly placed it on top of the rising pile. When they finished, a small treasure glistened under the bright bulb.

The doctor walked back to the table, drew the corners of the handkerchief together, and handed it to the jeweler. "You have your gold."

By coincidence the medal was presented to Bob on my birthday. The ceremony was simple and eloquent, and the medal a jeweler's work of art. Its inscription read:

"Token of friendship and gratefulness, this medal accompanies all the hearts of Cubans who love democracy." It was a birthday I shall remember.

In the days of the Cuban crisis, when Russian missiles were discovered on their launching pads in Havana, communication between Washington and Miami was continuous. Tension mounted in south Floridians, for they knew they sat just ninety miles from a potential tinderbox.

Troops moved through the city toward Key West; Civil Defense planning went into full operation. As Mayor, Bob was expected to assume unexpected duties in the event of attack. He attended meetings with other officials to quietly formulate plans, and hoped it would not be necessary to put them into effect. His city car appeared one morning equipped with red light and siren; he was a given a destination point, a command headquarters, to reach, should it become necessary. Most frightening of all to me was a mimeographed sheet delivered by messenger, a list of succession in the event one or all members of the Commission met with death.

Only one incident marred the effective planning in which Bob took part, and unfortunately, it stemmed from his own household. The list of succession arrived in the morning. Already nervous, I lunched with a group of equally nervous friends. On returning

The Beginning

home, I found a message from Bob saying he would not be home for dinner, did not know when he would be home, because of an emergency meeting.

The children went to bed, the maids, Angie and Zoila, retired, and I tried to forget the succession list by watching television. Suddenly the night was shattered by the wailing of sirens, at least a dozen. Over their screaming din rose one with a funny kind of warble, one I'd never heard before. I walked to the window to listen more closely; the city was *alive* with sirens. And in the distance, over all that noise, I was certain I heard the drone of planes.

Oh, no, I thought, it can't be!

I glanced quickly at the TV, back again at the black sky. The funny, warbling siren reached a crescendo; the TV program, still in progress, was not interrupted to tell everyone to take cover, but suddenly I knew we were being attacked—and those poor people at the television station didn't.

I became something resembling an IBM machine that had popped its wires and started punching all its cards, but remembered vaguely some past programming. I awakened Angie and Zoila, dragged my sleeping children out of bed, herded everyone downstairs to a hallway outside the linen closet (my spinning mind decided this was the safest place in the house), grabbed a blanket from the shelves and flung it on the floor, pointing to it as I gasped, "Down! " in English and Spanish. All this in a minute and a half. Not, I thought.

Bobby mumbled, "What'sa matter with you, Mom?" while Angie and Zoila began to cry and pray in Spanish. But I wasn't through.

I remembered a past Civil Defense course, and with the calmness of approaching insanity dashed out the back door for the electrical switch boxes. My arms resembled a churning windmill as mind raced. I'll never see Bob again... wonder where he is... darn him... have to save my family... why don't our neighbors turn off their lights?

I turned off the gas main too. Another safety precaution. Amazing how, though consumed with fright, a programmed mind remembers. Racing back to the door, I wondered if I would make it inside before the bomb hit. I did.

I told Angie and Zoila to be calm, after all, I was calm. Slowly, a deadly silence settled outside. Where were the planes? What had happened to the sirens?

At this point the programmed apparatus begins to wonder if it has been fed the wrong information. Just to make sure, I decided to call the Police Department. My question was phrased very carefully.

"We have been hearing some strange sirens, and we were just wondering if an air raid is in progress? " I was sure he heard me, but there was a silence on the other end of the line.

Then, a tired voice. "No-o M'am, what you heard was a new electronic siren on the Chief's car. They're just movin' troops through the city." As an afterthought, he added, "If it wuz an air raid, you'd be dead by now."

I sent everyone back to bed and finished going through the windmill procedure with the lights moments before Bob came home. He headed straight for the refrigerator, a gas refrigerator, and stopped.

"The gas is off! "

"Oh, ha-ha-ha! I turned it off! Guess what happened."

He said he was sure he couldn't guess, so I told him. At the end of my ragged recital, I casually mentioned calling the Police.

"Good God! I hope you didn't tell them who you were! "

I would have died first.

CHAPTER FOUR

The Decision

It was three o'clock in the morning. I awoke to find Bob pacing the floor.
"What's wrong?"
"I don't know, Faith. I just feel sort of funny."
I couldn't see his face in the half-dark but sensed the distress in his voice. I felt his forehead, and it was cold and clammy. "Let me take your temperature, Honey."
His body temperature registered ninety-six degrees.
"Bob, do you have pains anywhere?"
"No. I have a strange sensation in my jaw, though. It's not exactly a pain. It just feels funny."
"Come and sit down for a minute." I was trying to be casual, and taking his hand, I let my thumb wander toward his wrist; his pulse was slow and strong. Suddenly realizing I didn't know how fast or slow it should be, I felt my own; at least I could compare them. Mine was twice as fast, so I assumed a danger signal.
"Let's go downstairs for a few minutes," he suggested. "I feel like I need fresh air." He donned robe and slippers and headed rapidly for the stairs.
"Wait!" He looked at me questioningly.
"Well, you don't have to charge down!" I laughed, so arm in arm, we slowly descended the stairs.
Under the light, his naturally sunburned face was pale. There was a heaviness, a tired-weight look, in the way his arms hung at his sides. I remembered a medical article. "Bob, how do your arms feel?"

"Oh, okay, I guess." He rubbed one of them. "The left one feels a little tired."

The left one. That went with the article. "Look, I know this will sound silly, but why don't we drive to the hospital? Just, oh, you know, a quick check."

"Oh, no. I'm all right." But his voice lacked conviction.

His forehead was as damp as if he had stepped out of a shower, and I laid my hand on his cheek. It was icy.

"I'll be back in a second." Upstairs, I threw on clothes, not bothering to look but reaching for the nearest things at hand. Hurry, hurry. I knew little about medicine, but something was terribly wrong, I knew that.

"Come on, Honey. Just some fresh air," I said, dangling the car keys. Bob followed me slowly.

I started the motor, glanced at the instrument panel.

The needle of the gas gauge was on empty.

"Where are you going?" Bob asked, as we swung madly in the direction of the highway.

"Oh, to an all-night service station. We need a little gas."

"For Gods' sake, slow down! You're going to kill me getting me some fresh air!" He smiled, but it was a ghost of his usual grin. He sat slightly hunched, his arms clasped tightly in front of him.

"Are you cold?"

"Just a little."

We pulled into the service station, got a fast dollar's worth of gas, pulled out. I lit a cigarette, and Bob said, "You know, I feel like I don't ever want another cigarette!"

"Why? Are you having trouble breathing?"

"Well, a little. Not too much."

I pressed the accelerator harder.

"Faith, what the hell are you doing? Where are you going?"

"To the hospital." He didn't protest and that frightened me more. Hurry, hurry. My leg shook on the gas pedal, and there was nothing I could do to stop it. We raced in silence through dark streets, ignoring red lights. Bob looked at me but said nothing.

"Uh!"

"What's the matter?"

The Decision

"Nothing. Little pain. Nothing."

Oh, God, why is he talking like that, in jerky little phrases? And yet, I knew.

Next morning, Miamians read, MAYOR HAS HEART ATTACK.

Sophisticated Miami responded. Churches and civic groups all over the county held prayer services; a shopping plaza marquee, all advertising removed, stated, "A prayer for our Mayor;" English classes cancelled the day's lessons, and students wrote get-well letters instead.

Prayers reached the right address, and doctors said Bob would recover from the coronary occlusion.

Doctors Hospital was not so fortunate. It would be several weeks before switchboard operators enjoyed a leisurely coffee break ("Mayor High's condition is listed as satisfactory, Sir." "No, ma'm, Mayor High is not allowed visitors."), before nurses rested from reporters' questions. And it would be a while before the hospital recovered from the excitement of a huge flower arrangement from the White House, nurse's aides asking, please, might they have just one petal?

Word reached Bob in the hospital that a planned racial demonstration, a peaceful one, had been cancelled; Negro leaders felt it would be unfair while the Mayor was ill. It was a significant step.

Miami had been fortunate in race relations, but quiet activity on the part of a handful of men in the white and black communities was largely responsible for the good fortune. Bob felt a civic responsibility to all Miamians, black or white; they elected him, they deserved leadership. As a man, he felt a moral responsibility. If any one characteristic distinguished him, it was his humaneness; all men are entitled to respect, he believed, and fairness.

Before insurmountable problems sprang up, he called meetings with community leaders, black and white. For the first time in his life he shied away from newspaper and TV coverage; these were quiet, unheralded get-togethers with almost a furtive quality. Too much exposure might play on emotions, creating problems where there were none; he wanted integration of public facilities to come about with normalcy, with no fanfare.

One meeting was designed to open lunch counters, especially in department stores, to blacks. Department store executives, several ministers and members of the NAACP, and Bob, discussed the issue. One executive, president of a large downtown store, was adamantly against the proposal.

"But Mr. ——," Bob said, "You of all people could set the pace. Others will follow." It was an appeal to the man's vanity, well-known in business circles.

The executive scoffed. "Mr. Mayor, I'm in business to make money. We all are! This is strictly a matter of economics, and—I hope these gentlemen will understand," he nodded toward the black ministers, "I may as well be blunt. If we open our lunch room, we can write off thousands of dollars' worth of business."

"But what about our business? " one of the black men asked quietly. "You do not turn down our money at your sales' counters."

There was a silence.

Bob stood up. "Gentlemen, whether you like it or not, for whatever reason, I am here to tell you, It—is—coming!

"Frankly, I had hoped we could resolve this question on the basis of its rightness." He paused. "Let me tell you what I saw the other day."

He told them of stopping in a drug store for a hamburger; he was sitting at the counter, cooling off in the air conditioning. It was sweltering outside. A black man came in, holding a little girl, two or three years old, by the hand. He walked up to the counter to buy a coke, but the clerk said, "I'm sorry. I can't serve you."

The black man had walked in proudly, smiling at the little girl beside him. Now he dropped his eyes, a quick humiliation crossed his face as he glanced at the child. Raising his eyes once more to the clerk, he asked softly, "Could you just give me a glass of water for my little girl? " It was almost a plea.

The clerk filled a paper cup. "You'll have to take it outside."

Bob looked at the faces around the table, one by one, until he came to the executive who had protested. "I ask you, gentlemen, is that right? "

The man met his hard stare. "Perhaps we can work it out." He smiled. "After all, our company has always been a leader. I believe

The Decision 51

your words were, 'set the pace,' Mr. Mayor? " It was a beginning.

Integration of city-owned swimming pools came about in the same manner. Bob received a call from a black leader that two black youths were on their way to a pool located in an all-white section; they were going to test the new ruling. Bob quickly called the pool manager so he would be ready.

The youths were admitted with hardly a glance, and when they saw they actually could swim if they wanted to, they turned around and quietly left.

Because of Bob's age, thirty-nine, mildness of the attack, and general physical condition, his heart healed rapidly.

The first couple of months after the attack, he enjoyed extra hours with our children, now numbering five. There were Bobby, Holly, Cindy, Valerie, and—"Mayor has Fifth, Gets a Little High" read the headline—Bonnie Lou. Our growing family made a larger home necessary, so three bedrooms had given way to a sprawling, white-columned Colonial, set back on a sloping lawn. During the early weeks of recovery Bob was confined to the second floor, and a constant trooping of visitors, business associates, and secretaries with papers, reactivated his itch to be moving, to be back in action. The temporary restrictions made him fidgety.

Recovery forced time on him. Time to think, time for where-do-I-go-from-here thoughts. He was still a young man; barring something unforseen, his health would soon be as vigorous as before; he would preserve that health by using better judgment in the future—no more eighteen hours a day. But preserve it for what? For his family, of course, and because he loved life; to be an attorney; to be Mayor. But he had those things already. Most of all, he was a man who had to have a challenge; it was as necessary to him as air.

His political future seemed stable enough. He had given the Mayor's job everything he had—the heart attack was proof of that, he thought with a chuckle—and he was fairly certain he could be reelected the next time around. He was a popular mayor, his followers were devoted; in some quarters, however, his enemies were more fierce than before in their dislike for him. Because he was Robert King High there was no middle ground.

Once, a local politician accused him of being a "headline grabber," and he answered with an innocent, "Who, me?" The twitch at the corner of his mouth was a dead give-away to his thoughts. Sure, I'm a ham. Which of us in this profession isn't? But he loved the profession.

He had been offered a post as ambassador to a Latin American country, but he turned it down. Now, with recovery imminent, he was offered another. He gave it serious consideration. Though a successful attorney, an ambassadorship would impose financial obligations he could not assume; on the other hand, it was a distinction few men achieve; it would be an education for his children; it might take him away from some of the tensions which led to his heart attack, away from the rat race. But he liked the rat race.

The Magic City would be a hard place to leave. "I feel like I'm needed here," he said. "There's something—something else for me to do."

With mixed emotions he declined the post, and in so doing, signed his destiny.

An idea had been forming in his mind. At first, it seemed preposterous. It still did, a little. Yet, why not? The idea grew.

Bob never would have dreamed he'd be sitting in this spot, aboard Air Force One, the Presidential jet.

The plane lifted smoothly into the clouds above Tampa; soon it would reach Miami. A snappily-dressed aide approached Bob with a summons. Would he be good enough to come to the President's cabin?

Delighted, Bob entered compact yet elegant surroundings, blue rug with golden eagle and thirteen stars, easy chairs. Comfortable. As he and the President talked, he almost forgot that for the moment, this was the nerve-center of the world. Almost.

It was an informal visit, "just the two of us," Bob said later, with a touch of pride. It was November of 1963, and Kennedy was on a Florida speechmaking swing; naturally, their talk was political—the President's chances in Florida, how good or how difficult it might be in the next election.

"Well, we'll see what the papers do with us tomorrow," Kennedy said, a half-smile on his face. "Tell me, Bob, what about you? You don't plan to be Mayor all your life, do you?"

Bob said he didn't think so, as a matter of fact, he'd been doing a lot of thinking lately. He told the President his half-formed idea.

Kennedy listened, nodding slowly. All of a sudden, he grinned. Hell, he thought it was a great idea! It wouldn't be easy, but Bob ought to give it a try. He was for it all the way.

The two liked a challenge, and as they talked, a flicker of new purpose grew in Bob's eyes.

The seed was planted in fertile soil at an early age. The boy Robert couldn't get enough of Jefferson, Lincoln, and Robert E. Lee tales.

The seed was watered by Mayor Abe Aronovitz. After Bob's election, he watched his protegé in action, noting the interplay of emotion between Mayor and people. Bob was in his element in a throng, plunging into a crowd, grinning broadly, gripping outstretched hands. He didn't have to force a smile or handclasp; it was already there, eager to be received; and in return, the people gave themselves to him. It was like a feeding process, one nourishing the other.

"You know, Bob, you have the makings of a statesman," Mr. Abe remarked one evening. "I believe you can someday be governor of this state."

The watering process had begun.

Under the influence of John F. Kennedy, the seed took root. Within days after the conversation aboard Air Force One, an event occurred which rocked the world, an event that had a profound effect on the life of Bob High. It was the assassination of President Kennedy.

Bob was one of thousands who flew to Washington to mourn their fallen leader. In the small hours of the morning, he sat in his hotel room talking with a friend. There were many long silences, for he kept remembering a conversation with another friend only a few days before, somewhere in the clouds between Tampa and Miami. He had reached a half-way decision with that friend, and now that man was gone.

So it was that a black-draped Washington, beating to muffled drums, confirmed Bob in his decision. He would run for governor of Florida.

CHAPTER FIVE

"Hey, Look Me Over!"

The Florida Governor's chair offers a four-year tenure, but 1964 was a special two-year term of office. In 1963 the voters passed a constitutional amendment which provided for the election of the governor to a special two-year term in '64, returning to the regular four-year term in 1966.

The amendment came about to eliminate holding gubernatorial elections in the same year as Presidential elections; members of the Democratic Establishment in Florida believed Republican state victories could be minimized if not tied to national elections—and Florida had gone Republican nationally in 1951 and 1956. The amendment also provided that the man elected governor in 1964 would be given the unique opportunity to succeed himself in office.

In politics, the state was tradition-minded. Two states in one, Florida—north and south— in geography, economy, industry, and philosophy. Traditionally, north Floridians had the reputation of a built-in distrust for anyone from the Gold Coast, especially big Miami; established standards said that a candidate needed a huge war chest to run a statewide campaign.

The Mayor of Miami was out to shatter traditions.

Bob's entry into the governor's race resembled his first campaign for Mayor. By political standards the words "financial shoestring" were a kind description. Miami had adopted an ordinance that a candidate for city office could not spend more than $10,000; Bob carried this thinking into the governor's race, saying,

Dade County Headquarters for the gubernatorial race of 1964 on Flagler Street in Miami

"Public office should not be for sale to the highest bidder."

The temptations were great. A man in Vero Beach offered a donation of $25,000 with a slender string attached. He wanted a race track concession. In his hand was a cashier's check, and he held it up for Bob to see.

Bob stared at it. He had visions of television commercials, full-page newspaper ads; and at the moment, his campaign fund had three hundred and fifty dollars. He took the check then handed it back.

"Just wanted to see what it felt like," he said. "I'm sorry, but your money has some dirt on it."

Another similarity with the first Mayor's race was Bob's wildly enthusiastic supporters. They referred to themselves grandly as members of "the organization," but realists would have called it Hysteria, Inc. Housewives, stealing hours away from home, manned the headquarters in staggered shifts; businessmen, on their lunch hours or after work, dashed in for car-top signs, out again to distribute them; neighborhood children who were old enough to lick stamps contributed their part; even the little ones begged bumper strips for their tricycles. Friends knocked on doors, made telephone calls, typed letters, addressed envelopes, gave out literature at shopping centers; and when election day rolled around, they would scrutinize the polls and watch the poll-watchers.

A newspaper wag called the High organization a "campaign contraption charming in its innocent confusion!" Confusion was a compassionate word. Bob sometimes traveled as much as a thousand miles a day aboard a ragged and rumpled DC-3 that continually amazed everyone by getting off the ground. All over the state he urged integrity in government, while the polls and political pundits figured him to come in sixth out of a field of six candidates. The average voter would have said the same thing. So a small army of dedicated volunteers chipped away at the wall of Big League politics, and the pollsters kept laughing.

This was the year of the Civil Rights Bill when every politician did a soft-shoe routine around the question. But Bob High would not have been Bob High had he done so. Never mind that the bill was controlled by the Federal government, not the State; it was a moral issue, as well as a legal one, and he was in favor of it. As a candidate, the people had a right to know how he felt.

He had a speech coming up in Pensacola, red-neck country it was said, and he needed some advice. He called his editor-friend, Bill Baggs. Could he drop by the house?

"Be there in an hour," Baggs replied.

Baggs used to see Bob as a young attorney in the drug store of the DuPont Building, but the first time they met to talk at length was when Bob, the new Mayor, called to ask questions about civil rights. He realized the novice politician was concerned with issues, not votes. It was the beginning of a long friendship, and now, during the governor's race, they met every two or three nights to discuss what needed to be said, not what should be said to win votes.

Baggs arrived at the house, eased his long frame and rumpled seersucker suit into a chair, and smiled. There was an air of perpetual relaxation about him that many times caught his detractors off balance.

"What's up?"

Bob told him his life had been threatened. The threat was delivered through a third party in north Florida, would be carried out at the courthouse in Pensacola, where he was scheduled to speak.

The preceding week someone had taken a shot at Editor Baggs while he was walking his dog. "What did you do about that?" Bob asked. "Did you call the FBI, or did you let it go?"

"Hell, I let it go! I'd do the same thing, if I were you."

Bob grinned. "Will you help me draft my speech?"

"Let's get busy!"

"We may as well lay it on the line, Bill. I want to tell the truth, whether I'm elected or not."

They treated it as a game, in a way, writing down words, wondering what would happen when Bob spoke them.

A week later, Bob stood on the steps of the Pensacola courthouse, facing a hostile crowd. He stared them down, giving them look for look.

"Segregation is wrong," he said. "It is evil and un-American."

He told them he wanted to explain what civil rights was, to put it in proper perspective. "Too long politicians have prospered and prospected on the race issue. This is no better than treason!"

The crowd shuffled uncomfortably. Only a few nodded in agreement; most looked at the speaker with cold, hard stares. But they all listened, and the bullet meant for him was never fired.

Once Bob said, "Just to live in the times we face will take the nerve of Nathan Hale, the vision of Woodrow Wilson, the strength of Teddy Roosevelt, the compassion of Abraham Lincoln, the stubbornness of Andy Jackson, the statesmanship of John Adams—and the guts of Harry Truman!"

From the beginning Bob and Baggs talked of trying for a higher level of politics. The courthouse steps of Pensacola was one place to start, and when it was over, Baggs said, "Bob High committed the most courageous political act in the history of Florida."

Baggs' paper, *The Miami News*, was the only daily in the state to support Bob for Governor.

As the candidate's wife, most of my time was spent on the Bandwagon, an innovation in Florida politics. Without gold-plated campaign funds, it was born from a necessity to capture imagination and, since I didn't like to fly, keep me out of airplanes.

Traveling through the state, our caravan made a strange sight: one station wagon filled with six young mothers (five friends who persuaded their husbands and found baby sitters for twenty-three children), luggage, and matching outfits; another station wagon bearing five musicians (piano, bass, drum, sax, and banjo), and bringing up the rear, a monster of a yellow truck, decorated with red, white, and blue signs screaming, "Vote for High," wheezing and grinding its innards as it struggled to keep up with the automobiles.

We rendezvoused with members of the High organization in each town, transferred from station wagons to truck by means of our open-air elevator, a hydraulic lift at the rear of the truck, and the Bandwagon, loaded with human cargo, paraded through the city, ending at a reception or tea or interview, or all three.

Since my traveling companions were not paid workers, hired to do a job, but friends donating their time and talents, it made the difference between an oily group of hacks doing a job because they had to, and a closely-knit group doing something because they wanted to. It was the difference between a spark and a bonfire.

Day melted into day and became one continuous, out-of-focus newsreel: racing up the highway, slowing down so the truck could catch up, arriving late, boarding the truck, playing music under the steaming sun, dashing for cover under a filling station when raindrops started to fall, in the cars again, racing, laughing, crying, joking, discussing reactions, collapsing in a motel at night, sometimes too exhausted to eat dinner, up at dawn, eating breakfast, and always, always late.

But what reactions to the moving mass of music and humanity. A group waiting for a bus on a streetcorner suddenly glanced at one another, suspiciously; no, their ears were not deceiving them, that was music coming down the street! They looked up, curiously, starting to smile. They had never heard of this High fella or a High road, but the music was mighty fine, and those young ladies surely were havin' a good time!

A barber stepped out of his shop, saw what the commotion was all about, waved his hand disgustedly in the thumbs-down tradition, but watched anyway; Negro children danced, snapping fingers and tapping feet in perfect rhythm, then raced pell-mell along the sidewalk after the truck; a businessman in a brisk trot looked surprised, and his hand jerked in a kind of unaccustomed salute. A young mother pushing a baby stroller waited at the curb; her baby waved and gurgled at the ladies waving to him; the mother looked as if she'd like to wave, too, and taking courage from her baby who was not yet inhibited, she did.

In more than 4,000 miles on Florida roads, our only disagreement was over directions. Bob once said of his parents, "Daddy says he and mother have not had a quarrel in more than half a century of marriage. He admits, though, that sometimes they have 'reasoned together' so loud they could be heard in the next county! " We reasoned together frequently.

"He said to turn left."

"He said to turn right at the third traffic light! "

"Well, was he counting this light number one, or the next? "

The wagonmaster, bandleader Jimmy Peck, earned our name for him, "Big Daddy." Rotund and smiling, he tried to keep us on the right highways, fussing at his charges, soothing jangled nerves like a mother hen.

We knew repercussions from Bob's precedent-shattering speech in Pensacola. Passing through a north Florida hamlet--not intending to stop, just passing through--our cars, well marked with car-top High signs, were greeted by a street cornerful of loafers with profanity and filth. Twenty miles up the same highway, the band members stopped at a small restaurant for a cup of coffee. Two minutes later they marched angrily out; the owner would not serve High workers. In still another town, motel owners holding our reservations told us how relieved they were our band members were white! They had been told we traveled with a Negro band. In the same town, a prospective voter sidled up to me. "My dear, I'm so-o-o glad you came. People said you were Cuban, and some said you were," and she lowered her voice to a whisper, "colored! "

Such reactions were few, and amazingly enough, the madcap Bandwagon, rolling to the strains of "Hey, Look Me Over! " was a tremendous success. When the last trip was over, we speeded south, toward the Gold Coast. We were tired and anxious to get home. Besides, election day was upon us.

All the odds were against Bob, he knew that from the start, and on the night of the first primary, by eleven o'clock, Haydon Burns, the Mayor of Jacksonville, ran well out in front. Scott Kelly, a contender from the center of the state, was some thirty

Mayor High making announcement in campaign headquarters, 1964

thousand votes ahead of Bob. The political analysts of the TV tube, the IBM vote-prediction machines, projected Burns and Kelly in the run-off.

"Don't count me out yet!" Bob said.

It was impossible, but suddenly a crazy thing happened. Big Dade County, the largest of Florida's sixty-seven, was late, but it was finally making its voice heard. It way saying that the IBM machines were wrong. Its home-town boy, the fighting redhead, was in the run-off.

Pandemonium set in, not only at High headquarters, but all over the state. The men who ask questions, study the answers, and call the results a poll, were red-faced; back room politicians were stunned; voters who pulled the lever for High, certain he didn't have a chance but liking him anyway, were just as surprised.

The next three weeks developed into the battle of the Mayors, for Bob and Haydon Burns were mayors of the two largest cities in Florida, Miami and Jacksonville. Bob tried, unsuccessfully, to get Burns to agree to TV debates, for the High camp could not afford television time. The race ended on more steam than money.

Again, the pollsters predicted Bob to come in last. This time, they were right. But at High headquarters on election night, his supporters cheered until they were hoarse. A funny and uncommon thing to do. For some reason they believed he could be elected governor the next time around, two years. By shattering precedents, his defeat took on the guise of victory, for who had really believed a young man from the mountains of Tennessee could ever become Mayor of the Magic City, much less Governor of Florida?

Bob High believed it, and he said so.

Two days after Bob's defeat forty men from all over the state, area and county campaign managers, journeyed to our home. No longer amateurs in the political arena, their months of pitched battle led them to one determination: they were ready to think about the 1966 race. Because of the special two-year term, the 1964 election was the beginning of the '66 campaign for those who planned to run.

They had no question that Haydon Burns, the Democratic nominee, would be elected Governor in November, six months hence. His Republican opposition was minimal, and in nearly a century of Florida elections, winning the Democratic nomination was a surety to becoming chief of state.

Watch Burns closely, the managers said to Bob, and keep your name before the public. Next time we'll win.

During the succeeding eighteen months Bob spoke frequently throughout the state, but his travels were not limited to Florida. A situation of major import to Miami took him to New Jersey.

Twenty-five cities across the United States were seeking one franchise for a pro football team, offered by the American League. In June of '65 at an AFL meeting in Monmouth Park, New Jersey, it was rumored that Miami and New Orleans had the edge.

Officials of the League had told the Miami Mayor to stay away from the meeting, but he didn't listen; the outcome was vital to his city. He grabbed the News Director of the City's Publicity Department, caught a night flight to New Jersey, and the next morning requested permission to appear before the group.

Bob wanted that franchise for Miami and had taken the calculated risk. He presented the Miami story to them, including everything from driving time to the stadium to the average age of each community. The gamble paid off.

AFL Commissioner Joe Foss candidly admitted that the owners admired the Mayor's interest in pro football—and his nerve. So the Dolphins came to Miami.

Coinciding with the birth of the Dolphins was our own addition. Our sixth, Susan Jill, with flaming hair and navy blue eyes. Her birth brought new excitement for Bob, and impending decision. If he was going to enter the 1966 Governor's race, he had less than six months to make up his mind.

By now we had discussed the possibility many times, and next to the incumbent Governor, I was the biggest stumbling block. It wasn't easy to dismiss his heart attack, but he had just completed extensive examination and was in excellent health. As far as campaigns went, I would have preferred they didn't. But I could not ignore their existence.

"Just this one, Honey," Bob said. "If I lose, that'll be the end of it. I promise!"

Bob began to watch for political signposts that would tell him his chances. The first signpost came.

Governor Burns had become a powerful chief executive. He was sponsoring a $300 million road bond, and it would go on the November ballot for the voters' approval or rejection. Using every means available, the Governor pushed its acceptance.

Bob opposed it. The people of Florida would have to pay $113,000,000 in interest on the $300,000,000 loan, and he took to the trail, becoming a major spokesman against the road bond issue.

"This is nothing but a political plum," he stated, "thrown hurriedly together for political reasons."

That same November election held another test. Bob was running for reelection to his fifth term as Mayor, and he was concerned over voters' reactions to him after losing the '64 gubernatorial race. Human psychology was inclined to cast out a loser.

He had three opponents, and large sums of money were being spent to insure his defeat, thus insuring his nonpresence in the governor's race.

By the night of November 16th both tests were answered. Bob won reelection by almost two-to-one and set a record in the process. Never before had a man been elected to five consecutive terms.

More significantly, on the night of the first primary, November second, the voters showed their disapproval of the Governor's road bond issue. They overwhelmingly rejected it.

That meant Burns could be beaten.

Reporters pressed Bob. "What about it, Mayor? Does this mean the governor's race now?"

Bob promised a statement within a few days. First, one matter was left to dispose of. The intimation of an appointment for Bob as Ambassador to the Organization of American States.

He met with Bill Baggs to talk about it. "Guess who dropped by the other night?"

"I'm afraid to try! Who?"

Bob named a local attorney. "He brought word from——(a Washington senator) that if I would stay out of the governor's race, I was assured of being appointed Ambassador to the OAS."

"Well, well, that's very interesting," Baggs replied. "What do you say we make a few well-placed phone calls?"

They discovered that a high-ranking person in the State Department had in his possession a letter which gave him the authority to approve the OAS appointment. They also ascertained the gentleman would never approve Robert King High.

"Bob," Baggs said, swiveling away from the telephone, "I'm afraid the senator is trying to sandbag you into staying out of the governor's race."

"I think you're right."

Bob telegrammed his reply. "In regard to the important matter we discussed recently, I find I will be unable to accept such an appointment at this time. I appreciate your interest in this regard."

The next day Bob called the papers. They ran an announcement that "Mayor High will issue an important statement on Saturday morning, November 27th."

Saturday morning.

The cameraman, an early arrival, stood on the second floor balcony of our home, adjusting a light meter. He had an excellent vantage point to capture the view of a sloping lawn almost hidden by three hundred people. Bob originally planned to announce his candidacy over a hundred-station radio hook-up, but the legality of spending funds before the official qualifying date (February 15) was uncertain. He decided to make the announcement from our home.

Many of those who stood in the morning sunshine carried placards left over from the '64 campaign; some sipped coffee while greeting 'old' supporters they hadn't seen for two years; others joined Jimmy Peck's band in the chorus of "Hey, Look Me Over." They were excited, and it seemed as if I was watching persons who had suddenly been reborn.

A wooden podium was centered on the brick floor of the veranda, covered with microphones and cables. Seated nearby were Bob's sister, Martha, who worked in his law office, and his parents, just down from Chattanooga. At Daddy High's appearance, hand-clapping spread through the crowd, for during the '64 campaign he became a great favorite. He beamed with embarrassed pleasure, raised a hand in greeting. The seventy-seven-year-old wonder was ready to hit the campaign trail once again.

At exactly ten o'clock Bob emerged from our home and stepped to the podium. A great roar went up from the crowd.

"I am in this race," he began, "because I am deeply troubled about the direction our state government is taking.

"There must be a new mood in Florida government. A mood which rejects the philosophy that 'to the victor belong the spoils.' Such a policy has no place in our state, in the government which belongs to the people.

"The 'buddy system' must be replaced by the competitive bid system."

The crowd was intent, hanging on each word. Cameras grinded away.

"The City of Miami has had an honest, efficient administration," Bob continued "free from any taint of corruption." The people interrupted with sustained applause.

"I pledge to conduct myself in the same manner as Governor of Florida!"

The cheering rose to an insane frenzy, and as the candidate stood there, a faraway expression crossed his face. It was the same expression I had seen when he stepped off Air Force One in 1963.

CHAPTER SIX

The Campaign

The lobby was empty, its only occupants a quiet guard and a janitor pushing a broom. On this Sunday afternoon in December the new Ferré Building seemed hollow and eerie, intensifying my feelings of dread.

Most people were at home, catching a nap or busy with holiday plans and all the other things I wished I were busy with. Instead, I was accompanying Bob to his law office to attend a highly confidential meeting that would plan his campaign for governor. I felt out of place, certain the men who would be there, most of whom I had never met, would think I belonged at home. But Bob wanted me with him.

Our footsteps echoed behind us, bouncing from the cold marble floors, following us into the elevator. Bob pushed the button marked "ten" and waited impatiently for the doors to close. Superficially, he looked like a young man on his way to play a round of golf, veering off course long enough to pick up a forgotten paper at the office. To one who knew the signs, however, the drumming of restless fingers and the preoccupied expression in his eyes disclosed racing thoughts and a mind ready for decision.

We got off the elevator, turned right, and paused outside heavy panelled doors. The gilt lettering, HIGH, STACK & DAVIS, announced more than a long-awaited move to new offices; they told that the red-headed attorney from the country had made a place in the big city and the world of law. Bob looked at me with a boyish smile.

At Miami's Torch of Friendship (with Vice President Lyndon B. Johnson, Senator Claude Pepper, City Commissioners Sidney Aronovitz and Alice Wainwright)

We entered the reception room, footsteps muffled by deep blue carpeting. Its flow to the inner offices was interrupted in the hallway by a tweedy and sickening coral, partial payment from a client who had it left over from a hotel carpeting job. Feeding into the inverted-U hallway were offices for the attorneys, cubicles for the secretaries, a library, storage closets, and a huge conference room whose book-lined walls were in sharp contrast to the empty bookshelves that once faced the gambling young lawyer.

The glassed corner of the receptionist, and at the right-hand corner of the U, a closed door lettered *Mr. High*, the murmur of voices. Bob opened the door.

The panelled office with its giant expanse of glass overlooking Biscayne Bay belied a quiet Sunday afternoon. There was Bob's half-moon desk, littered with papers as usual; walls were hung with photographs of Bob with Jack Kennedy, one with now-President Lyndon Johnson, the usual lawyer's degrees, and an antique Gilbert clock that had just chimed the hour of two; a stereo unit rested mutely against one wall, and opposite it was the conversation area—tan leather couch, easy chairs, large coffee table—buried under ashtrays, coffee cups, and paper, paper, paper.

Half a dozen men, in sport shirts or with ties loosened under starched collars, looked up.

"Well, well, look who's here! "

"There he is! "

"Good afternoon, Mr. Governor! "

They pushed more chairs into the circle, casting polite or welcoming or slightly baffled glances at me. The welcoming smile came from Bob's campaign manager, whom I had met before.

"Sit down, Faith," he said, holding a chair. "Nice to see you! "

Don Petit, slight, intense, dark-haired, was a professional campaign manager. A former newspaperman, he was a veteran of political wars, an expert in the mechanics of a campaign. He and Bob had long been casual friends, but one evening in Washington over dinner, the two discussed a closer relationship. Don was with the Office of Economic Opportunity program, but the challenge of a battle against all odds brought him back to Miami, his former home.

Professionals were working with Bob now, drafted in what resembled an old-fashioned game of tag. Bob engaged the campaign manager; the campaign manager rounded up two specialists in political research; the researchers recruited two more, the cover editor of *Look* Magazine and a free-lance photographer who handled special assignments for *Life*. An exception to the piggy-back acquisition was speechwriter Don Wilkes, a former college mate of Bob's who had called and offered his services.

"Well, are we ready to get down to work? " Bob asked.

"Hey, what do you mean? " Petit chuckled. "We've been at it since last night! "

"Okay, okay! I admit it was the wrong choice of words! That's where you'll come in, Wilkes," and Bob nodded at the speechwriter.

"I think as good a place as any to begin is with our theme," said Petit. "We can go from there."

The man from *Look* passed a folder to Bob. "This is how I see it," he smiled.

The proposed brochure. On its cover was a sketch of Bob's face, remarkable in likeness; printed at the top were the words "THE ISSUE IS—and across the bottom, in bold letters,—INTEGRITY."

The Campaign 69

"It looks great! "

"Here, Bob," the photographer spoke up. "We thought this picture should be used on the cover."

"Where did this come from? "

"You don't know what we've been through to find it—we must have looked at four hundred pictures! Anyway, remember when President Kennedy was in the Orange Bowl with the men from the Bay of Pigs? Well, a news photographer took a shot of the two of you on the platform. It hit us! I cropped your face out, blew it up, and—," with a shrug he indicated the glossy photo, a full-face of Bob, squinting slightly in the sun. Whether squint or reality, his face held a determined expression.

"I think it's a good choice," Bob said. "How about the rest of you? " Six heads nodded in agreement.

"It's an excellent photo, Bawhb, but if we might get back to the theme—don't you feel the word integrity has been rawther overworked these days? "

The question came from Don Wilkes, the speechwriter. He would have stood out in any group, not so much for the freckles and bright red hair, nor for his imposing manner, but for diction that seemed as remote from south Florida as the blank verse of Shakespeare would from a Disney movie. The well-modulated voice echoed with England, Oxford, and the tragedy of Hamlet, as the speaker considered each word, weighed it for effect, allowed it to roll across his tongue. Wilkes was an American by birth, but he was Shakespeare in the High organization.

"Oh-h, I don't know," answered Bob. "I think integrity is a pretty good word."

"We haven't heard from the lahvly lady at all. Faith—may I call you Faith? —don't you agree with me? "

"What do you think, Honey?" Bob turned to the others. "She has an instinct for those things! "

Now why did Bob have to say that! Fascinated with how a campaign was organized by experts, I had begun to relax, certain that the men, deeply involved in their discussion, had forgotten my presence until Wilkes' question to me. I felt like a butterfly about to be impaled.

"Well, since you asked—I like it. I think it's perfect! "

That did it. Wilkes glanced at me mournfully and Petit said, "Hear, hear! " Bob winked.

Discussion followed and *Life* volunteered, "You know, Wilkes may have a point. Integrity has been bandied around an awful lot."

"Precisely! " said Wilkes. "And in my humble opinion, we do want to avoid cliches."

Petit took a positive stand. "There's one point you may be missing, Don. Integrity is something people are concerned with, and it affects every phase of government.

"Also, Bob's whole career gives meaning to the word. The clean-up drives, his insistence on insurance bids, everything! Integrity sums up the man, the ideals—it's like a solid base underneath all the hoopla of a campaign."

One of the researchers, Bill Haddad, leaned forward. "Every campaign needs one major issue to hang its hat on." Black-haired, with the aura of unbridled energy, Bill had been Inspector General with the Office of Economic Opportunity program, the number two spot under Sergeant Shriver. After leaving the program, he and a deputy from OEO formed a research consulting business in New York. "Integrity and Bob High are practically synonymous," he stated emphatically. "It's a natural! "

"I'd have to go along with Bill on that," smiled the other half of the research team. Bob Clampitt was the antithesis of his partner: he had sandy-colored hair, a perennially youthful face, a deceptively shy manner. "To me, THE ISSUE IS INTEGRITY is our big umbrella over all the other issues in Bob's platform."

The question was settled, and Bob reached into a briefcase, pulling out a thick, black binder. "Here's one thing more," he said, handing it to Wilkes. "This poll indicates people are concerned with integrity in government." Bob and Petit exchanged glances.

"I didn't know you'd had a poll taken, Bahwb."

"I didn't! But the opposition did, and a friend made a photostat for me. Needless to say, this is confidential."

Wilkes looked at the page Bob marked. "My Gawd! This is dynamite! "

The poll showed Governor Burns in comfortable position, rated high on competency; Bob was strong in name identification, integrity. The dynamite, however, was reflected in the question, "If the governor's race were held today, for whom would you vote?"

According to the poll, Democratic votes would be cast in the following proportions: Mayor High, 34%; Governor Burns, 28.5%; Scott Kelly (a contender from '64), 18.5%; Undecided, 19%.

"You're leading Burns! " Wilkes was incredulous, and with reason. The incumbent Governor, with the tenure and power of office, should have been far ahead of his challengers.

"Which brings up another point," said Petit. "This may help us get financial backing. You know, the people who are willing to help if they think they have a winner."

Political campaigns mean fund raising. Bob found it disagreeable and for the most part, left it to aides; but even a well-intentioned aide could make mistakes. In the '64 race an attorney from central Florida, known to be involved with bolita operations, offered Bob a donation of $500. Bob refused, but the attorney mailed his check to Miami anyway, and an unsuspecting aide deposited it. Fortunately, the mistake was discovered, the check mailed back. But Petit was right; many persons would not consider contributing to a campaign, no matter how qualified the candidate, if they felt he did not have a winner's chance. I expressed distaste.

"I know, Faith, but there are such people," Don grinned wryly, "and in politics you have to be practical."

Don outlined their financing plans. They would rely heavily on individual contributions; the usual letters and calls requesting aid would be sent, businessmen's luncheons, amply supplied with blank checks, held. "The seed money—the foundation— will come from organized labor," he said.

National labor, especially railway unions, had taken an interest in Bob because of his work in trying to settle the volatile FEC strike. The powerful DuPont interests, who owned and operated the Florida East Coast Railway system, were controlled by financier Ed Ball, and Bob aligned himself with the striking workers. By the time the strike was settled, Ball had become the common foe of both the railway workers and the Mayor of Miami.

"There are local unions," Petit continued, "who have special campaign funds set up, and it is from these funds our seed money will come."

Labor was not the only national group watching the Florida Governor's race. Florida, the ninth largest state in the union, was a southern state northern in character, and its importance to the national political scene could not be minimized. While the national Democratic Party could not and would not take sides in state primaries, there were national Democrats who were pulling for High, offering advice.

"Ned will be finance chairman, right? "

"Yes, and he'll keep a tight purse, too! " Bob chuckled, describing his law partner's caution. Ned Davis, a towering ex-football player, gave the appearance of rock-bound reliability. And he was that, Bob added; his methodical nature would serve him well as finance chairman. Bob's other law partner, Bud Stack—young, extroverted, and a JFK look-alike—would travel with Bob.

There would be no Bandwagon on Florida highways this time, and Petit turned to me. "Will you be traveling with Bob very much, Faith? "

"Yes-s. Whenever possible."

Bob explained my hesitance. "She doesn't like to fly. I've given up getting her on a plane! She usually drives with several friends, has to leave home a day or two ahead of me to get there on time—"

"Oh, Bob! "

"—and when she arrives, she lies about how fast they drove and what good time they made! "

We all laughed, and Bob plunged in again. "Let's get to the issues. Bill, you've researched the generic drug business. What do you have? "

It was Bob's contention that generic drugs were chemically the same as trade names but less well-known, and therefore inexpensive by comparison.

"First of all, this should have definite appeal to the senior citizen living on a limited budget." Bill explained that a huge amount of money was spent on advertising trade name drugs, so of course they cost more; doctors normally prescribed by trade names, and the druggist was required by law to provide medicine as stated on the prescription. If the patient was aware of this and desired it, however, his doctor ought to prescribe by generic terms.

The Campaign 73

"In many instances," Bill concluded, "the generic drug was 1000% cheaper! "

Bob whistled. "If the average person knew that! "

"It'll be your job to see they do! "

"Right! Now, as I see it, these are the things we want to go with. Wilkes, since you're the speechwriter, you'll need to know the issues as well as I." Bob began ticking them off.

Education bumped along a rocky road, leading toward what appeared chaos. Teachers' salaries were inadequate; old buildings needed repairs and improvements; educators estimated that Dade County (Greater Miami) alone would need 1,200 new classrooms by 1970. Bob was assured of substantial support from educators and college students because he offered an optimum platform containing ingredients the academic community wanted for quality education. From textbooks to buildings, his was the classic position.

The only negative aspect, one the opponents would be certain to use, was the cost. It would be staggering, an additional burden to the taxpayer. Well, this was the taxpayer's choice, Bob said, but he offered other sources of revenue to finance the plan. A severance tax on the phosphate and minerals industry in Florida. A four-percent sales tax on everything but food and medicine. Elimination of waste and inefficiency in government, amounting to hundreds of thousands of dollars per year.

The tax base should be equalized, he said, so that individual home owners and small businessmen would not be saddled with their taxes and those of big business, too. He would point out how much money the City of Miami saved by putting its insurance business out for bid. The state government, with enormous insurance contracts to award and many another apple to threaten Eden, could also ignore the ancient and corrupt 'buddy system' and award contracts to low bidders. The only decision had to do with morality.

Bob once told an audience of young people, "We must apply to each question which faces our governing bodies a certain formula: measure every decision first against the standard of morality. If it meets that standard, it will meet all standards."

Bob looked at Wilkes, who was taking notes, and added another item. He would push for legislation to establish a strict code of ethics for public officials. "In short," he concluded, "the issue has to be integrity!"

"Bravo!"

"Damn right!"

I remembered an incident at a recent luncheon with leading businessmen of Jacksonville. One, a life-long Republican, backed Bob into a corner.

"Mayor High, why should I vote for you, a Democrat and a liberal?"

"I don't know what you mean by liberal," Bob replied. "In fiscal matters, I am a conservative. In human matters—if you call fairness being a liberal, then I am that.

"As to why you should vote for me, a Democrat—well, I like to think I have integrity."

The man reflected a moment, then smiled. "I believe you'll have my vote."

I pulled myself back to the present, and Petit was explaining some of the mechanics of the campaign. In addition to the thousand-and-one pulls on a campaign manager, Don would oversee all scheduling for the candidate, from speeches to TV appearances to appointments with editorial boards of Florida newspapers, seeking their support. Petit would have a staff of twenty under him, and they would rent the thirteenth floor (ignoring superstition) of the Ferré Building for use as State Headquarters; they would lease or borrow office machines and furniture, he said, and would have an expert in radio and TV.

Part of the fifteenth floor would be used by Haddad and Clampitt with their volunteers, numbering around forty. The two men were specialists in negative research, Petit said, and went on to explain what he meant by the term.

"There are two areas of research in a campaign. Positive research, or what the candidate stands for, and negative research, the opponents' record on issues, and rebuttal to what they may say about you!"

Haddad and Clampitt would also advise on the design for literature, the best way to illustrate Bob's issue positions, and the use of mass communications.

Campaigning in rural Florida

Campaigning in 1966 with his father, "Daddy High" (in front of Mayor High, with hat on)

"This will be, primarily, a mass communications campaign as opposed to an organizational campaign.

"Governor Burns has a tremendous organization, the influence of office, unlimited funds; Scott Kelly has a large organization, and he too is healthily-financed. Meanwhile, our candidate here," he smiled at Bob, "has neither powerful organization nor big money. Which means we'll have to get the most mileage we can out of every dollar we spend."

They would allocate the bulk of their funds for television, purchasing half-hour blocks of statewide TV time as a substitute for organization. In many cases, one person to meet Bob's plane at the airport was the organization in that area! Hopefully, mass communications would draw others into the network.

Bob's home base organization, his Miami supporters in nine years of mayoralty races, was the cornerstone. A cross section of persons from every walk of life, it would be the initial base now, and they'd look for the same kind of support in other large counties.

"Who knows? We might even have a chairman in all sixty-seven counties by the end of the race! "

"One thing I'd like to get the concensus on is the 'Feller from Flat Creek' item," Bob said.

He referred to a recent article whose title alluded to his birthplace, Flat Creek, Tennessee, and the suggestion that a reprint be distributed in north Florida, where many thought of him as a big-city slicker.

"Sounds like a lotta corn to me," somebody muttered.

It imaged a man rurally-oriented in his thinking, another added, and this was not so. Bob was the mayor of a metropolitan city with accompanying urban problems—streets, highways, conservation, to name a few.

"Let's hold it on the fire," they finally decided.

"Well, as far as the 'flaming liberal' tag the red necks hung on me in '64," Bob said, "I guess if anyone can dispel that picture, my daddy can." Daddy High was going to travel north Florida, visiting every city and hamlet, and anyone who met him would have a diffucult time believing his son was a slick politician from the wicked city.

"Frankly, I'm not particularly worried about that aspect," Petit stated. He felt their best position in north Florida would be to accept the situations they knew existed and get the maximum mileage possible out of what they did have. There would be a three-way split in the rural areas, most of the votes going to Burns and Kelly; the High forces would simply get what they could.

As for Bob's image, if a man's philosophy and actions can properly be termed an image, it was already established. Name-identification was present, as a result of the '64 race; he was known to be a Democrat all the way. Outside of Florida, the product of his crusades, expertise in Latin America, and even his friendship with JFK, gave rise to the picture of an urbane mayor in an urban city.

In Florida, if any one event established Bob as an effective voice in state politics, it was the recent road bond issue. As a probable contender for the Governorship, he was also the only figure of statewide prominence to speak out against the road bond until its defeat at the polls, a bitter blow to the Governor.

"I'll tell you, Bob," said Petit, "The road bond issue was the road to the Governor's chair for you."

Because of Bob's image, because of the issues he would raise, and because of the planned mass communications attack, there evolved a campaign strategy. It was based on simple mathematics.

The statistical picture of Florida showed that forty-seven counties had only 17.7% registered Democrats; the remaining twenty counties, mostly urban in nature, held a whopping 82.3% registered Democrats. Against Burns and Kelly, two strong conservatives who could be expected to split the forty-seven counties, Bob's course was clear. He would go for the twenty urban counties, the 82.3% and his platform would reflect a sensitivity to his support in these areas.

"Well, I guess that about wraps it up." Bob said. "Thanks a lot, all of you."

"Don't thank us yet! " Petit cracked. "Right now our aim is for you to be the Democratic nominee. Then you can thank us and mean it! "

There were stretches and yawns and shuffling of papers, and finally everyone said goodbye. For a while.

No more the "charming and innocent confusion" of the past. This was 1966 and the professionals were turning new pages; some would parallel the old ones; others would be different; and not a few would be distinctly unpleasant.

There were six candidates in the governor's race: Democrats Governor Haydon Burns, State Senator Scott Kelly, Tallahassee pollster Sam Foor, Mayor Bob High, and Republicans Claude Kirk and Richard Muldrew. Qualifying day opened at noon, February fifteenth, in Tallahassee, the state capital.

Qualifying day dawned gray and gloomy, shrouding the state buildings in a flat mist. The famous Florida sun was somewhere in hiding, the sparkling golden capitol dome barely visible, but Bob refused to be gloomy. Officially, this was his big day.

The High Flier, a DC-3 carrying a hundred persons from south Florida, was on its way, and others were motoring in from all over the Panhandle. I was astonished, for in the '64 race if a dozen persons from northwest Florida, the Panhandle, had declared themselves for Bob, we would have demanded a legal holiday.

Bob and I raced from our hotel in separate directions; he, to before-noon meetings with aides, my friends and I to nearby Monticello, where we would join a motorcade of High supporters. The motorcade would enter Tally—the natives' irreverent name for Tallahassee—just before noon, terminating at the capitol building.

At our rendezvous point, a large drive-in theater, we spied Daddy High, just off a plane from Chattanooga. He was surrounded by a group of well-dressed men and women.

"Hello, there! "

"Well, well, well! Hello, hello! " And to the group with him, "Here's my driver! "

"Do you trust me to get you to the capitol in one piece? "

"I reckon so! Look at this crowd, Faith! Different from the last time, isn't it? "

It was. As far as eye could see, cars, some two hundred of them, stretched out to the highway, lined up in motorcade precision. People intermingled all along the line, chattering, waving High signs, pasting bumper stickers on their cars, passing out crepe paper streamers. There was excitement in the air, undampened by hovering rain clouds.

"Faith," Daddy High whispered, "I think he'll do it this time! "

His face, alive with happiness, was tinged with awe and pride in his son. A walking ad for the fountain of youth, he was one of his son's biggest assets. Daddy High was from the hills of Tennessee, and as far as I was concerned, he was the hills of Tennessee, the vanishing American of another era who plowed and tilled the soil, who remembered to say grace before meals, and who closed a contract with a handshake rather than a piece of paper.

"Okay, everybody! Let's go, let's go! " The motorcade director hurried people to their cars. Doors slammed, horns honked, streamers waved.

The caravan flew low along the highway. Even I had trouble keeping up with the lead car, and my passengers, Daddy High in the front seat and Pat McDonald in the back, smiled grimly at the speedometer. Near the city limits of Tally, I missed the ashtray and dropped a lighted cigarette on the floor. It promptly rolled underneath the seat.

"Daddy High, would you please see if you can find my cigarette?" I asked, easing up on the accelerator.

Daddy High sat, unmoving. I finally realized I had spoken into his 'bad' ear, as smoke began curling up from under the seat.

"Pat, do something! "

She did. In a flash, she plunged over the back seat, her derriere raised to half-mast, hand scrabbling along the floor. Daddy High jumped, thinking Pat had lost her mind instead of my cigarette; the car in back of us started honking. It was an impressive entry into Florida's seat of government.

I met Bob pacing buoyantly on the steps of the capitol. "Look at all the people, Faith! The rain didn't keep them away! "

It was noon. Turning into the building, we led supporters and an entourage of newsmen down the halls, to the office of the Secretary of State. The Secretary's office was jammed with onlookers, and hot TV lights ate up what little oxygen there was. While cameras whirred, Bob filed the necessary papers, paid his fee, signed his name, and it became official. He was running for Governor.

Cheers, handshakes, a pat on the shoulders, flashbulbs popping. Bob was jubilant, responding to supporters' emotions with quick affection, heading back down the hallway toward the capitol steps where he would deliver his qualifying speech.

Daddy High

paused, clutched my hand. His face came close, shutting out the crowd around us, and he whispered, "The next time we stand here, I'll be Governor. I feel it! " Then, "Are you ready? "

I nodded, but after the mechanical brevity of the filing procedure, I was ill-prepared for the sight ahead of us. The veranda, large as it was, could not accommodate the mammoth crowd that shuffled and grunted and bumped and apologized, as individuals scrambled to line the steps or get a position on the lawn's front row. The several hundred were jostled anew by High Flier passengers, who hurried out of airport buses from across the street.

Bob stepped to the podium, arranged his papers, and the television cameras began to zero in. One technician shushed the crowd, while another, eyes riveted on a stop watch, arm poised in the air, was ready to give cue. Five fingers up, five seconds to go. Three fingers. One. His arm shot down, finger pointed at Bob.

"How I came to this place and this occasion makes the unbelievable believable," Bob said.

Several heads nodded in agreement, notably Daddy High's It was easy to read his thoughts: his boy, not long away from scarcity and little opportunity, and he was running for Governor of Florida. His eyes glistened.

"May I quote," Bob continued, "from an article in this week's *Saturday Evening Post* entitled, 'Crisis in State Government,' and sub-titled, 'The Octopus in the State House.' 'Greed, laziness, inefficiency, waste, stupidity . . . are (among) the many forces that have been strangling and bankrupting our state governments.'

"What is more ominous is that the article cites Florida, repeatedly, as illustrative of the worst in government morality." His right arm chopped down for emphasis.

" 'Easy morality,' and I quote, 'is the prevailing morality in the government of Florida.' "

The crowd was attentive, alert to every intonation in his voice, ready to respond, and Bob, sensing their mood, drew strength from them. The few sprinkles widened into a steady drizzle, and there was a hushed rustle as umbrellas began to dot the scene; strangers moved closer to strangers, sharing an umbrella or a raincoat or a newspaper; plastic bonnets sprouted on newly-coiffed heads.

"In Florida we verge on government of the politicians, by the politicians, and for the politicians. This may be good for the politicians, but it is not at all good for good government."

The crowd appeared mesmerized by the vigorous speaker with the chopping right arm. The woman with garish make-up, her jaw working in cadence with Bob's speech, had finally given up trying to push her way in front of the camera and was listening carefully, continuing to chew her gum; the man sporting a top hat wound with "High for Governor," waved a white-topped cane in the air for applause and occasionally jabbed the person nearest him to show his approval. Young men and women from Florida State University, who either had no classes or cut the ones they did have, stood listening as if to a respected professor; their faces mirrored the susceptible emotion of youth.

With an almost imperceptible surge, an intake of breath, the people sensed their candidate was winding up.

"The issue in this campaign is integrity in government." Bob's face was stern. He seemed oblivious to the cameras, aware only of an inner urge to make himself understood.

"Integrity in government, as I intend it to be understood as the issue in this campaign, means NON—POLITICAL POLITICS.

"If the fight is worthwhile, the cause good, now is the time to enlist.

"The state we have to save is our own."

The cheers told him he was a full-fledged candidate.

CHAPTER SEVEN

Under the Sun

Jacksonville. On the banks of the St. Johns River. A different city, where the river flows north. A big city, trading its wares at a sprawling seaport. Thirty minutes away is the oldest city in the United States, St. Augustine, but it has left no particular mark on its neighboring metropolis. Jacksonville seemed a stepchild of Florida; with moss-hung oaks, ante-bellum architecture, and a matching philosophy, I always thought its natural mother should be Georgia.

It was named after Andrew Jackson, the first territorial Governor of Florida, and Bob quickly reminds everyone that Jackson, like he, was a native of Tennessee. Jacksonville was also home base for Haydon Burns before his election as Governor; he had served as its mayor, so this was "his" city. To the High forces, stepping through a field of land mines was easier than working for Bob High in Jacksonville.

Comfortably settled in a hotel suite, it was difficult for me to remember that outside politics lay like a waiting panther. We had left the crowds at the state capital in time to reach Jacksonville by dusk, and although one person was missing, he would join me tomorrow.

A hotel employee's whispered warning told us our rooms were bugged. Here was Adventure, and my friends and I searched unsuccessfully for a hidden microphone, tapping baseboards and everything else in sight.

"Hm-m-m," Sally said. "They must think we know something!"

We laughed about our detective work with the Bruces and the Terrys, intimate friends and coordinators for Bob's campaign in Jacksonville. The two couples had joined us for dinner in the room, and easy conversation was a bridge to the eleven o'clock news. We were anxious to hear a re-cap of the Qualifying Day ceremonies, especially the newscaster's interpretation in this, Governor Burns' stronghold.

"By God! " boomed Don Bruce, "two years ago it took us a month to find half a dozen men who'd allow their names to be linked publicly with Bob! Things look better this time, but it'll still be one helluva fight! "

"He just must win," Jenny drawled. "I can't bear the thought of his losing! "

How strange was life. Each of us had been a most unpolitical person until the advent of Bob High; it seemed natural to compare our present anxiety with the sport of a vacation two summers ago.

Bob and I, with Jenny and Herman Terry, were on our way home from the mountains. I was taking my turn at driving—nervously, because my driver's license had expired.

"For heavens' sake, Faith, get that thing renewed as soon as we get home," Bob ordered. "If you don't do it within a month, you'll have to take the test over."

"I could pass it again! "

"Ha! " Bob found an appreciative audience in the Terrys. "Hey, there's a drug store up ahead! Stop for a minute so I can get a cigar."

I pulled into a parking space across the street from the drug store, and Bob hopped out. "Anyone want anything? "

"No, thanks."

We were in a small Georgia town, quiet and sleepy on this July afternoon.

"You know, there's something about a small town. I think I'm a small-town girl at heart."

"I know what you mean," Herman said. "Look at that! " He pointed at a small boxlike structure edging the sidewalk; it was about four times the size of a phone booth. Inside a policeman sat in air-conditioned comfort, reading a newspaper.

"Why, it's a booth for the police! That's a nice idea."

Under the Sun

Suddenly the telephone rang in the booth, and we saw the policeman lift the receiver, glance across the street, and begin talking.

"I wonder what on earth is keeping Bob," I said. "I wish he'd hurry!"

Because there was nothing else to do, we watched the officer, a rotund gentleman in his fifties, leave the booth, cross the street, and enter the drug store. In a few minutes he returned, and with a casual glance in our direction, re-entered his booth.

"For a second I thought he was going to come over!" I breathed. "If he had asked to see my driver's license—I wish Bob would hurry!"

Finally Bob emerged from the drug store, engulfed in a cloud of smoke, and crossed to the car.

"What were you doing, picking the tobacco?"

In our attention to Bob, we forgot about the policeman. He was striding purposefully toward the car.

"Good aftahnoon, young lady."

"Oh! G-Good afternoon." I was sure I had G–U–I–L–T–Y written across my face.

"Mighty hot aftahnoon, isn't it?"

"Yes, yes. It surely is." I would have agreed with him if he had said it was a cold night.

"You know, we've got a habit around heah. Whenevah we see an outa state car, we always like to ask foah the driver's license. It's nothin' but a sorta custom. May I see yoah's?"

"S-Surely. Jenny would you hand me my purse please?"

I swiveled toward the back seat and held out my hand for the purse. As our eyes met, I knew she understood my silent plea for help, but there was nothing she could do short of eating my old driver's license. My eyes swept Bob. He was trying to wipe a concerned expression from his face, or so it seemed.

"Here it is," and I handed the license out the window.

"Why, ma'm! This driver's license ain't no good! It's expiahed!"

Suddenly Bob leaned across me. "Oh, it's all right, Officer! I'm the Mayor of Miami," he said pompously. "I'll take care of it!"

Oh! I stared at Bob, willing him to catch my what-has-happened-have-you-lost-your-mind look. He ignored me.

"It will be all right, Officer," he repeated. "I'll see that it's taken care of!"

"We-ell, so youah the Mayah of Mahami." He strolled around to Bob's side of the car. "Ah've always wanted to go theah. Mighty pleased to meet yuh!"

They shook hands. "Ah guess we can foahget about this if the little lady'll promise to renew it when she gits home!"

"I'll see that she does."

As we drove away, there was dead silence. For a minute.

"Bob, how could you? You sounded so... so... ooh!" I suddenly recalled the officer's words, "an out-of-state car." "He couldn't have known we were from out of the state; he was standing in front of the car—he didn't see the Florida tag! BOB HIGH!"

The back seat came to life with howls, for Herman had suspected all along.

"What are you talking about, Honey?"

Bob, the picture of innocence, turned widened blue eyes on me. A tell-tale flush across his face admitted what he would not until a month later; his sudden inspiration, a quick phone call to the officer in the booth, a meeting in the drug store to explain his plot.

"But he didn't know you! What if he hadn't agreed to play along?"

Bob shrugged. "Oh-h, I don't know. He looked like he had a sense of humor!"

What a carefree time that had been, and now, here we were—three of us from that trip, anyway—talking about politics and bugged rooms and Bob's qualifying speech.

"Bob used a word incorrectly! We'd better tell him tomorrow so he won't make the mistake again."

Mildred Bruce was a schoolteacher, so we all looked at her with respect. "What was it?"

"Precedence. Bob said 'pre*ceed*ence,' but it's *pre*cedence, with the accent on the first syllable."

We rolled the word around and around until it sounded like an alien mumble and finally decided to consult Mr. Webster.

"Ha, ha, Mildred! You're wrong!" Don looked at her over his

glasses. "Here it is, all spelled out. Bob was right! In the future, will you please keep your comments to yourself?"

Our laughter was interrupted by a knock on the door, and Herman rose to admit a familiar figure.

"Well, well," the caller said, "ladies, Don, Herman--How are you all? Good to see, you Faith."

Gene LeBeuf, darkly handsome with black hair and brows, sat down and began to munch on a left-over roll. "Looks like I got here just in time to hear what good ole Jacksonville has to say about our favorite candidate! We're in the hop spot here!"

Gene was a roving trouble-shooter for Bob in northeast Florida; he had been with him in the '64 race, and though short on diplomacy, he was long on loyalty. Glancing at his watch, he reminded us it was nearly eleven.

"Come on, come on! Let's get the old television working! Faith doll, how've you been?"

After a minute of fiddling with knobs, the TV crackled to life. Conversation faltered. Our eyes and ears concentrated on the beginning newscast, and someone's "here it is!" brought instant quiet.

"And now, turning to state news," the announcer's voice said, "and long-awaited events from the capital. Miami Mayor Robert King High was expected to qualify for the state's highest office today in Tallahassee, but when the noon hour ended, he had not yet arrived."

"What?"

"Well, I'll be damned."

"Did you hear that?"

We were incredulous, staring dumbly but not mutely at the TV. It was unthinkable that a television station, operating for the sole purpose of informing the public, would distort or ignore the truth. Or lie. We felt cheated, completely betrayed.

"So that's how it's going to be, is it?" Gene raged.

A cry went up to call the station, and he was the first one at the telephone. Angrily stating the purpose of his call, he was told to hold the line until the broadcast ended.

"That'll be too late! I want a correction now!" His bushy eyebrows jumped to an inverted V as the robot-like voice on the other end of the line repeated he would have to wait.

When the newscaster finally came to the phone, Gene told him that, among other things, he had egg on his face. The announcer promised the station would retract.

"You sure as hell will, buddy! " He slammed down the receiver, scowling, "That yo-yo! "

The word yo-yo, depending upon how Gene used it, was either complimentary or withering. We had no trouble deciphering his intent this night.

"How could they? " Jenny moaned. "How could they? "

The next day we greeted Bob with our disturbing report. He was visibly shaken, for even though the station had promised to correct the story, he knew the damage was already done.

There was more bad news. Herman told him how two aides had visited a well-known liquor baron, demanding money for the campaign. The man had previously offered financial aid, and Bob declined it. Luckily, Herman found out and stopped the transaction in time.

"My own people! " Bob was aghast. "What are they trying to do to me? "

Among Bob's own people in Jacksonville, there were many new faces, many old ones from '64. One man in evidence again was something of a character, an honest-to-goodness one-of-a-kind, who boasted he had never worked a day in his life. In spite of this astonishing statement, he worked vigorously in politics and knew everything that was going on everywhere. It was said of him in Jacksonville, "We'd rather have Ed on our side than against us!"

One time, we were not so sure. Bob and I were visiting the Terrys, prior to the 1964 election, and awakened early one morning to an urgent call from Ed.

"Bob? The Roosevelt Hotel is on fire and Haydon Burns (then Mayor of Jacksonville) is down here with the fire department, getting his picture on TV! Come down right away! "

Bob said thank you, but he didn't think he ought to do that. We chuckled but thought no more of it until a newscast several hours later. The commentator's announcement left us thunderstruck.

"Mayor Robert King High of Miami, a guest of the hotel, has been taken to the hospital. It is believed his condition is not serious."

Ed was determined, one way or another, to get his candidate some free publicity! And now, two years later, Bob's Jacksonville supporters still said the same thing.

"Rather have him with us than against us! "

Back in Miami, Bob wrestled with an old monster: prejudice. Because of ill health, one of the city commissioners resigned his office, and it became the task of the remaining four to appoint someone to take his place.

In the previous November election, Mrs. Athalie Range ran for one of the city commission slots, making the run-off but losing to her opponent by a narrow margin: therefore Bob thought she was the logical choice, in addition to being a well-qualified one, to fill the vacant seat. If Mrs. Range was appointed, she would be Miami's first black commissioner.

A local attorney, also a black and a supporter of Bob's, pressed for his own appointment. He argued that if Mrs. Range was being considered, he too should be.

"You're missing the whole point," Bob told him. "I'm not considering her because she is black. She ran for the job in November, and she happens to be qualified." He did not need to add she came within a thousand votes of winning.

Politicians are subject to pressure as long as they hold office, but the influence peddling over this appointment was no ordinary kind. Bob's office admitted visitors who had other names to push; I took messages at home from callers with self-righteous protests. The occasions were exceptional only because complainants stated a common end: "But Mrs. Range is a Negro! " Even Bob's black attorney-friend practiced a reverse discrimination.

The night before the city commission meeting that would resolve the question, campaign advisers visited Bob. They were edgy, fearful of repercussions in the governor's race. They too had been under pressure, getting calls spotted around the state, urging them to persuade Bob to find another appointee; this one was too dangerous, they said.

"This is no longer a city question. It's a moral one," Bob said.

But he was concerned. He argued with his aides, and finally, he argued with himself. He was not naive; he had been around Florida politics long enough to know this incident might cost him the election. He was ambitious; he wanted the governor's seat, and it was only a step away unless. . .

Unless what? He finally said to himself and his advisers. The answer was painful in its honesty. Unless he ignored his conscience.

The men left, nodding slowly, and Bob and I went into the kitchen for a cup of coffee. He looked haggard. I wondered if the pain in his eyes was not so much for himself as for the demon that lies within man.

Suddenly the phone rang. It was a long-distance call from an adviser in north Florida, hoping for an eleventh hour change in Bob's decision. It was easy to fill the blanks in his conversation.

"Mayor, are you still going to appoint Mrs. Range?"

Bob's face tightened, his hand ground the point of a pencil into the table top. "Yes, I am. And I have a commission majority to go along with me."

"Mayor, I hate to tell you this, but, well, you know how some of these Crackers are. About a dozen of them have threatened to pull out of the campaign if you do this."

"Well, the hell with 'em then!"

As he slammed down the receiver, the grinding pencil snapped in half.

With the appointment of Mrs. Range, and no mass exodus from the High campaign, Bob flung himself into preparations for his campaign kick-off, a giant rally in Miami's Tropical Park race track. More than anything, he was concerned with the weather.

Politicians are funny. They are affected by the weather because the weather makes people stay inside or drives them out, and since the lot of the politician is in the hands of the people, they like to feel they have a fighting chance with sunshine.

Unlike the drizzly day of qualifying, the Sunday afternoon of the kick-off made scholars of the men who write ads for the chamber of commerce. Puffy clouds scudded across a blue sky, and the beaming sun matched Bob's mood.

Tropical Park was alive with people. It was difficult to imagine race horses, led by jockeys in colorful silks, prancing around the turf. Instead of vendors hawking their racing charts, volunteers

Under the Sun

pushed a different commodity: Brochures reminding us "THE ISSUE IS INTEGRITY," bumper stickers splashed with "ELECT BOB HIGH GOVERNOR," or "IT'S HIGH TIME" buttons.

The giant parking lot was a scene of bedlam. Sunburned volunteers, dripping with exertion, waved cars into available spaces shouting, "Over here, sir," or "Look out, lady! " and "Don't forget to vote for High! "

People wore High buttons on shirt or blouse collars, on hats and purses. One woman had made the buttons into a pair of cumbersome earrings, and they dangled grandly, if awkwardly, from her ears. When the buttons gave out, there were always bumper stickers to be wound around straw hats and sunshades, or pasted across a dress, Miss America-style.

Children turned out in droves for balloons, rides on the portable merry-go-round, and free hot dogs. A sixteen-piece orchestra alternated with a Dixieland jazz band, filling the air with "Hey, Look Me Over" and "Moon Over Miami." The musicians sweltered gallantly in maroon jackets and bow ties.

No bugler blew the notes for the next race today; his spot facing the packed stands was occupied by a wobbly stage. Its wooden timbers creaked and strained under unaccustomed weight: Bob and I, our minister, campaign coordinators, public officials. But while the stage was wobbly, the candidate was not.

"Faith, can you imagine this many people turning out? "

His address to the crowd of some 20,000, more or less, depending upon whether one was cautious or spectacular, was received with cheers and whistles. He was relieved that a group of city employees seeking a pay raise had not staged their threatened "sing-in." In the commotion, they might have gone unnoticed if they had come!

The free food brought appalling sights. Hot dog and coke stands were surrounded by shoving, pushing gluttons; women, armed with huge pocketbooks and shopping bags, scooped up pounds of weiners or buns or both; one grabbed an armload of food, stuffed it into her shopping bag, then turned to a friend. "Why don't you take some, dearie. It's free! "

The wild ones were conspicuous from the vast majority, well-mannered families, out for a Sunday afternoon. There was enough of a mixture, though, to remind one of the greatest show on earth. I wondered if Mr. Barnum ever attended a political rally.

March lived up to its blustery name in more than weather. On the 15th, the *Washington Post* carried a column by correspondents Rowland Evans and Robert Novak that opened a hornet's nest.

The column, "Inside Report," said:

"A secret poll reveals that the political revolution coming to the Deep South is now well under way in Florida.

"The poll was commissioned by the campaign managers of Governor Haydon Burns, considered a cinch by professional politicians to beat Mayor Robert King High of Miami for a four-year term as Governor in the May 3 Democratic primary. The poll stunned the Burns staff, who sought to cover it up. It shows High, beaten two years ago by Burns, with a slight lead.

The secret poll of the Washington column was the same one "a friend on the other side" had copied for Bob. The black notebook.

Reaction from all three camps (High, Burns, and Kelly) was instantaneous. The Governor said he did not think such a poll existed and, if it did, it certainly did not come from the Burns organization as the story claimed; Kelly accused Bob of dreaming up the statistics for the poll; the High forces were smug. Bob's only comment was to propose that he, Burns, and Kelly share the cost of a new poll.

Like a snowball, the intrigue gathered momentum. In a story the following day, columnist Evans disclosed the name of the polling company, saying he was "told a Jacksonville food company paid for the report."

The president of the polling company said, "Reports of this kind are confidential. I will tell you that our survey was not financed by the Governor or his organization, but I will not tell you who did pay for it."

The snowball rolled on, with an astonishing development. Governor Burns charged that Senator Robert Kennedy was a moving factor in the High campaign, that the New York senator was trying to elect a governor in Florida. Signs of the Senator's connection with Bob, he said, included three campaign aides who recently had worked for Sergeant Shriver, Kennedy's brother-in-law: Don Petit,

Bill Haddad, and Bob Clampitt. The researchers, Haddad and Clampitt, were designated "ghost writers" for High.

Staff members took the charges lightly. "Ghost writers for High," they mused. "Hm-m-m, sounds like a song! "

The office of Senator Robert Kennedy promptly issued a statement denying the charge: "The senator is not getting into Florida politics. He's not even backing candidates in the New York primary."

From the campaign trail Bob said, "Despite all the stories you have heard about Bob Kennedy and his confederates, the truth is my daddy is the only outsider who has been active in my campaign! "

Governor Burns was not finished. He claimed the support of President Johnson and Vice-President Humphrey, saying there was "no question whatsoever" about the presidential support.

The next day, the *Tampa Tribune* answered: "Humphrey, White House Deny Backing Burns Campaign Bid."

By now names, as well as the Governor's charges, were being tossed around like balloons. Scott Kelly called Burns "Mr. Slick" and Bob a "good follower." Burns called Kelly a "desperate candidate" and Bob "that little candidate from down south." Bob called Kelly, who was heavily supported by the phosphate industry, "Fearless Phosphate."

News reporters, always on the lookout for color, were saying that present indications from the candidates pointed to a livelier-than-usual Governor's race.

In a political campaign, the press is as important as the candidates. What reporters and editorial writers say and how they say it will influence a vast majority of readers. To be effective a reporter must remain impartial and objective, no matter what his personal feelings, no matter how difficult. In the minority are newspaper hacks who slant a story, according to their likes or moods; the average newspaperman wants the truth—nothing more, nothing less. And the politician, if he has nothing to hide, wants the same thing.

Whether a politician knows it, a reporter sees him at his best and his worst. If he doesn't have the ingrained knack of sizing you up, he develops it. And when he does, look out! A professional judge of character is the good reporter, seldom wrong.

While innumerable politicians are honest and honorable, there are those who are neither. Like the child in the TV commercial who floats through the air in a plastic balloon, there are politicians who float in their own plastic world, seeing and hearing what they want to, not what is. A politician is surrounded by hacks, hangers-on, and yes-men, as well as his friends, and in the glory of the moment it may be difficult to distinguish among them, especially if he hears only the flattery or believes his retinue exists for him alone. A politician can become pompous, condescending to nod to the populace as if to bless them, and if he slips into this mold, no one knows the true man who lies beneath, least of all, he himself.

Some of our closest friends were members of the press, and we finally realized why this was so. The world in which Bob and I lived, the world of politics, was often void of reality, a glittering deception. Not so with the world of news; it demanded substance, and its people, for all their human foibles, were real.

With few exceptions Bob and press corps respected each other as men and as professionals, and after a period of sizing one another up, candidate High and newsman drifted into a comfortable rapport.

How many times I heard, "Mayor, what's the real story on this?"

"I'll tell you what's underneath, but can you hold up on it for a few days?"

"Sure."

Or late at night, a phone call. "Bob, I know it's late, but can you spare some information? I've got a deadline pushing at my heels."

He always had the time because he understood deadlines. He worked by them too.

Though some members of the press felt Bob was wrong in bucking trends, Jack Roberts of the *Miami News* said he was 50% reporter, and not many disagreed. "Like a reporter, he knows what makes news. He has an instinct for it. High's not afraid to comment on anything and he's not afraid to act—he knows the difference between right and wrong!"

Jack, a heavy-set man with unblinking eyes that hid their speculation, went to great lengths to obtain facts. Shortly after Christmas, 1965, he accompanied Bob to Mexico City on what the *News* called a "mission of mercy."

Wendall Rollason, a Miamian, was being held in a Mexican jail charged with faking passports for Cuban exiles. A man who tried to help the refugees get their families out of Cuba, he had taken $100,000 (collected by the Cubans) and flown to Mexico to secure passports. The money was paid, the passports never materialized, and Rollason was in jail on a trumped-up charge.

His wife, after months of exhausting regular channels, called Bob for help. So it was that Bob and Jack caught a plane for Mexico City. They arrived late at night, and first thing the next morning, they went to see the American ambassador.

The Ambassador was angry. "I resent your interference, Mayor High. Things are not done this way here! " Protocol.

"I don't care how things are done! We're trying to do what you should have done months ago! "

Bob and Jack stalked out and called on Rollason in his cell. He was a sick man, pale and emaciated, and at the sight of the two from home, he burst into tears.

"Mayor," he said, "there are no ethics here." He made it clear he was afraid he knew too much about Mexican politics.

Their next stop was the office of the head of the Mexican Supreme Court. The gentleman was not in, so unannounced, they went to his home. From there, they met with the Mayor of Mexico City, who greeted them cordially. They wanted to be certain Mexico knew that someone in authority in the U.S.A. was concerned.

The wheels were set in motion, but they turned slowly. It was nearly a year before Rollason was allowed to return home.

After sharing the foreign intrigue, Jack stated emphatically, "Bob High's a genuine article."

Florida newspapers sent representatives to travel with the candidates around the state, and the High plane was loud with clacking typewriters as men labored over stories and deadlines.

Many of the newsmen traveling with Bob were repeating the same experiences they'd had in the '64 race. They didn't need to prove their courage; when they stepped on a High plane, they took their lives in their hands!

One morning Bill Sweisgood from the *Florida Times-Union* in Jacksonville raced the forty-minute drive to Opa-Locka airport (the High planes rarely used Miami International because of a forty-dollar landing fee). Campaign personnel had scrounged planes from anywhere and everywhere, trying to accommodate the force of newsmen and aides, and by the time Bill arrived, the candidate was already in the air, winging toward Clearwater.

There was one plane left, one available seat on it, and two reporters--Bill and a TV man--trying to get aboard. They decided to flip a coin.

"Ha! You lose," said Bill. "You have to go! "

The unfortunate TV man turned to look at the plane and moaned. Slightly out-of-date, it had struts with wires holding things together.

As it wobbled hopefully toward the clouds, big letters painted on the side came into view: "JIMMY JONES, THE FLYING REALTOR." Later, Bill heard that the tired, old plane began losing altitude over the Glades, and at 600 feet above the ground the pilot found an emergency landing strip. The TV man returned to Miami by car.

The campaign found an old DC-3, the type called "gooney bird" in World War II. A unique paint covered the inside upholstery: the paint had never dried. On one flight a cry suddenly went out, "The Mayor's gone! " "Where's Bob? " After a moment of panic someone glimpsed a shoe sticking out from under one of the seats. The tired candidate was stretched out, sound asleep, on the floor. At least no wet paint was there.

The reporters tagged themselves "The Rumpled Retinue," and no one questioned how they got the name. They said they didn't file a flight plan, they filed a "fright plan." One proudly remarked, "I've been through six crash landings—three of 'em with Bob High! "

Traveling with Bob day after day, they came to know some of his speeches by heart. There was one story in particular Bob used so much they were getting sick of it.

"Faith has always tried to keep the children from feeling self-important because of my position," Bob would say, "and on one occasion she reprimanded our daughter, Holly--'You are not to say your daddy is the Mayor.'

Under the Sun 97

"The next day when Holly was visiting a neighbor's child," he continued, "the mother asked if it was true that her father was mayor.

"Holly solemnly replied, 'No. My mother said he wasn't my daddy!' "

This tale, coupled with an opponent's charge that Bob, as an attorney, had represented a meat packer accused of using horsemeat (true) and selling it to the schools (untrue), led the reporters to compose an original ditty.

Bill Sweisgood, Bob's choice as Poet Laureate of the group, dashed to his seat, grabbed pencil and paper, and scribbled furiously. In a minute they roused the sleeping candidate.

"Mayor! We've got a song for you! It's to the tune of 'Hello, Dolly.' " Roaring voices chorused:

"Hey there, Holly
I'm your daddy, Holly
No matter what your mommy tries to say.
Hey there, Holly
Eat your horsemeat, Holly
We feed it to our school kids every day!"

Bob doubled over but reacted quickly. He and a couple of aides went into conference in a corner of the plane and composed a song roasting the press.

Determined to have the last word, at the plane's next stop one of the reporters scurried to a grocery store and picked up a can of Hill's horsemeat. Back on board, they covered "Hill's" with "High" (cut from a bumper sticker), placed the can on a tray, and served Bob his dinner!

Traveling with Bob on a political campaign turned out to be, in the words of one, "an offbeat, incredible experience." The reporters, always exhausted from trying to keep up with deadlines and the candidate, were eager for any diversion. They concocted what came to be known as "the catechism of Bob High."

Bob had a standard speech they knew inside and out, and between landings the "catechism game" would begin.

"What is the issue?" a reporter yelled.
"Integrity is the issue!"
"What state have we got to save?"
"Our own!"

"When is the time to begin? "

"The time is NOW! "

Once, when all the questions in the catechism had been exhausted, a few of them got up a poker game. An unlucky reporter, having parted with most of his money, ran up and down the aisles, shouting hysterically, "Gambling on the High plane! Gambling on the High plane! "

The typing and the race for the telephone went on. So did the good-natured banter, the games, the poems, the sleepless nights, the endless shepherding from plane to car to rally and back again. The sharp-eyed group with pencils poised continued to write thousands of lines of copy about the man they had been sent to cover, dogging his footsteps, asking questions, exchanging confidences, watching him move through a crowd, noting the response of the people, probing his beliefs, and—reciting the catechism.

Out of all this a picture began to emerge. It was of men in the process of developing a closely-knit relationship, closing the gap between stranger and friend.

Now, when Bob fell asleep in the seat, somewhere between take-off and landing, the clacking typewriters slackened their pace, the voices lowered a degree. A reporter, quietly reminding the others that the candidate had suffered a heart attack a couple of years ago and didn't they think he ought to slow down, removed his jacket and spread it across the sleeping form.

It was a world of cementing that special man-bond known only to men; it was a world in which even I would have been an intruder.

This was going to be some race, the press said: writers were watching it with interest. I suspected some were watching it with their hearts.

CHAPTER EIGHT

Laugh Your Way Through Hell

Politics gets in the bloodstream, building a suspense that never quite goes away. Its public side emphasizes the toothy smiles, the hoopla of rallies, the jitters of opening night, the thrill of the chase after the elusive vote.

But the excitement, suspense, and public show represent one face of the political coin. The other is a side little known and little understood, except by those swept into the core: sometimes a political campaign seems more like a march into hell. No matter what the outcome nor the motives, politics draws from a person his best and his worst. To know a person's true character, some say, watch him when he gets behind a steering wheel. Or in a political campaign.

Anyone can be a politician; some men aspire to be statesmen. The folklore of politics is responsible for two cynical definitions of a statesman: "a politician who is held upright by equal pressure from all sides," and "a successful politician who is dead." The man who, in some cloudy vision of the future, dares to see himself as another Norris or Stevenson knows the achievement will be hard-earned, the physical and mental ordeals beyond belief.

Bob's typical day on the road, if any day was typical, went something like this: up at 5:30 a.m. to tackle a batch of messages, all marked "Urgent," a briefing by his aides in between shaving, showering, and dressing, a run-down on the day's itinerary, a swirl of hedge-hopping plane trips in anything that could fly, airport receptions and fast motorcades, mass meetings with cheers and handshakes and speeches, conferences with telephone calls and handshakes and speeches, two or three luncheons, shopping center tours on the run, more of the same for the second half of the day, with one or two dinners replacing the luncheons—dinners he either did not eat or didn't know he ate because of endless interruptions. Another speech or two, or maybe some television tapings. Then tumbling bone-weary into bed, eighteen or twenty hours after the day began.

A day in Miami ran much the same way. The only difference was that I, instead of a harried aide, handed him the messages. The aides were always downstairs waiting to check the itinerary with Bob. One hapless fellow made the mistake of tapping on our bedroom door early one morning.

"It's bad enough that I have to see your smiling face at my breakfast table every morning," I said graciously, "but don't you dare come in my bedroom! "

This brings up a trait of my husband's I found difficult to accept. I could not stand noise or smiles before at least two cups of coffee in the morning, but Bob, maddeningly, awakened with a happy grin. He sang in the shower, whistled while he dressed and bounded down the stairs into the kitchen.

There, he was greeted by cheery aides. "Good morning! " Good morning! "

"Here he is, bright and shiny and ready to go! "

"And here we are, ready to go with you! "

It was nauseating. I sat mumbling evilly into my cup of coffee, plotting what I would do to them all when the campaign was over!

The flesh of political man takes a terrible beating, but the physical ordeal was of secondary concern for it did not compare, terrible as it was, with the mental stress. For months on end, Bob was swept into seeing and meeting and getting to know thousands of campaign workers and voters. Gone was the familiar routine of everyday living; the family had only fugitive hours together. Sometimes Bob would fly home late at night, when convenience demanded he stay in the city he had just left, to be able to see the children the next morning for a few minutes, to be there when they tumbled into the bedroom.

Laugh Your Way Through Hell 101

"Daddy!" "Daddy's here!" "Dad!" The chorus greeted him when he was able to jet home for dinner. It was like a football huddle, Bob in the center of the circle, everyone talking at once, laughing, vying for attention.

And then, "Come on, Bobby! Let's pass a few!"

He'd grab a football and out they dashed, followed by a built-in cheering section. The tired lines around his eyes would disappear, miraculously.

"Okay! Let's see if you can catch this one!"

He played as hard as he worked, but it was clear the time was well-spent. During those brief hours he seemed to undergo a complete rejuvenation, and compressed as those hours were, I had to admit it was quality, not quantity, that mattered. Because there was so little time, the children did not receive an uncommunicative, "Uh!" from behind a newspaper they got the whole man.

"This is the worst part, Faith. The very worst," he would say, bestowing kisses of goodbye on stair-stepped faces. But it had to be done.

I had wondered if the racial overtones from 1964 were dead. No. They were merely stowed away, biding their time, for the hate-peddlers were about their grisly work again.

I stood there looking down at the sheet of paper in my hand. Filth. Worse, it was race-baiting, and by comparison filth was something cool, sweet, and clean.

Bob, in his usual early morning rush, had paused a minute at the door, as if trying to decide something. Finally he opened his briefcase, pulled out a sheet of paper, and looked at me with a strange expression, a cross between pain and nausea.

"You might as well be prepared for this, in case you run into it somewhere," he said, thrusting the paper in my hand. "They are handing it out in north Florida."

I recalled Sally's remark in Jacksonville, "They must think we know something!" She had sounded lighthearted, but now it was different.

The haters had done their work well. The "throw-away"—a bit of printer's ink on cheap paper, meant to be handed out, looked at, and thrown away—depicted a smiling black woman, sitting in a rocking chair, obviously pregnant. The caption underneath read: "I went all the way with Bob High! "

What kind of twisted mentality produced such hate? I shivered. A shadowy breed, sons and daughters of the night—the nameless, faceless, formless ones who traffic in hate and ignorance. The race-baiters.

As a public official and as a man, Bob believed in equal rights and opportunities for all; he considered himself a fair-minded person. Conservative. Liberal. Moderate. Brands of toothpaste, not people. But the sick minds grew restless, whispering the word "ultra-liberal," giving it the sound of a contagious disease.

When one of his workers in north Florida, where racial feelings were most sensitive, suggested Bob make a statement soft-pedaling the issue of segregation, he replied, "Look, I want to be governor. But not if I have to wear false colors."

Yet he wondered what other forms of madness the racebaiters would contrive. He did not have long to wait. Whisperers said Robert Kennedy was financing Bob's campaign, and a second "throw-away" pictured the faces of Dr. Martin Luther King, Senator Robert Kennedy, and Robert King High, on an open hand of playing cards. Its caption: "A poker hand—one joker and a pair of kings."

A couple of months before qualifying in Tallahassee, Bob drove to the *Miami News* building to visit a friend one Saturday afternoon. In an empty lot across the street from the paper, the newsboys' regular touch football game was deep in progress.

Impulsively, Bob asked, "Can I play? "

"Sure! "

Bob quarterbacked and his team won 6-0. He thanked the boys for the game, then went to keep his appointment.

A sharp-eyed reporter in the city room had recognized the new recruit and snapped some pictures. When Bob disappeared inside the building, the reporter came out to talk with the newsboys. "Hey, boys! Know who that was? "

"I dunno," one replied. "I think he's somebody works around here someplace."

"That was Mayor Robert King High! "

"That was him? No stuff? He plays pretty good! "

The next night the picture and a story appeared on the front page of the *News*. Bob chuckled that the little boys did not know who their quarterback was.

Now, two months later, copies of the same *News* picture, with newly-added invective, was circulating in north Florida. The newsboys were blacks.

As Jonathan Swift wrote, "The art of the lie was invented by the devil, but it remained for the politician to refine it and put it to uses too diabolical for the devil to contemplate."

We floated on a wild and violent sea, and it would get worse before it got better. The turbulence began a slow rise with occasional late-night telephone calls and muttered threats, or scrawled lines enclosed in an envelope. One writer, who at least had the courage to sign his name, sent a series of ugly letters to Bob at his law office. In a spurt of deviltry, Bob decided to answer them.

"Dear ——: Enclosed are a series of letters which some jackass has been sending me from time to time. He has been signing your name to them, and I thought you ought to know about it. Very truly yours, Robert King High."

The letters stopped.

The race-baiting had its effect on newsmen traveling with Bob. They didn't like it anymore than he did, but like the candidate from Miami, they kept their sense of humor. They had to.

One reporter, popular with the group, was pulled off Bob's campaign and sent to cover another candidate for a while. An avowed High supporter, his releases were as objective as he could make them, but according to his traveling companions, he hung on to his backwoods prejudices.

"A great guy, but prejudiced," a fellow reporter said. "Only one in the group who was—and he admitted it! "

With his absence there was a great gap in the Rumpled Retinue, and on the day following his departure, Poet Laureate Bill stood in the front of the plane to tell them about it.

"Hey! Listen, everybody! "

The deadline-beaters stopped their typewriters, Bob and his aides looked up.

"Now that our 'ole buddy has been sent to the other side, does anyone realize what that means? "

Several eyebrows lifted, mouths began to twitch. They knew something was coming.

"Tell us, o observant one!" a voice rang out.

"We've been left high and dry," Bill shouted. "We don't have a bigot anymore!" He was answered by appreciative chuckles.

"Do you realize what it means to have an entourage without a bigot? We'll be the laughing stock of Florida!" The guffaws were beginning to drown him out. "But never fear! I have a plan!"

"Tell us, o poet!"

"I have taken it upon my humble self to appoint one of our number to fill this gap. I therefore appoint you, Ev," and his finger shot toward one of the innocent onlookers, "to act as our official Bigot-in-Residence!"

The Bigot-in-Residence protested, "But I need a press secretary!"

"I," intoned Bill, "will be your press secretary."

So it was that, between hedgehoppings, while the plane bounced with men trying to shake off the dust of the campaign trail, the "press secretary" would leap to his feet shouting, "Attention! Attention!

"It's time to hear from our Bigot-in-Residence! Ev, say something prejudiced!"

The Bigot, in standard-bearer voice, shouted, "I have always stood two-square for equality! Whites living in white houses, and blacks living in black houses!" Mock cheers.

"You really should not call me a bigot," he said, looking hurt. "I hate only two things--and one of those is prejudice!"

Killing shrieks broke up the game until the next time. Because they were wise, they found truth in humor. And as one said wistfully, "You just try to laugh your way through hell."

The campaign began to take on a television-mystery aspect. Bob found taps on all the telephones. The office, the headquarters, our home. We could never take privacy for granted, at home or on the road. We managed to outwit them (whoever they were) at least once, with the help of a friendly room clerk.

Bob and I had driven to Sarasota, on Florida's west coast, to attend the State Legislative Conclave, arriving late at night and very tired. He was signing the register when the desk clerk suddenly leaned across the expanse of counter.

"Mayor High," his voice was a whisper, "I have taken the liberty of changing your room. It's not as nice as the one you were down for, but . . ."

"What's the matter?"

"Your room was bugged. I found out about it last night and hoped I'd be on duty when you checked in."

"I'm glad you were," Bob said. "I appreciate that."

Bob was not the only target during the campaign. My activities, and even those of our children, were noted in the copy of a detective's report during the '64 race. The man had been hired by another candidate, and when the election was over he had an argument with his employer, stalked out, and came to Bob's office. "I thought you might be interested in this," he said.

"This" was a copy of his detailed report on the High family's activities, when I went to the grocery store, what time our children left for school each morning. Because of the incident, this time, in 1966, I was ready and watching.

It finally happened. I began noticing a small white car, its only occupant a sun-glassed man, parked across the street from our home; wherever I drove, my rear-view mirror reflected the small white auto several car-lengths behind. I turned, he turned. I stopped, he stopped. Oh well, I thought, if he has nothing better to do.

A week of follow-the-leader went by, and one morning I pulled out of the driveway, intending to go to the grocery store. There was the little white car as usual, and seated behind the steering wheel, my friend.

I will play the secret agent game, too, I decided, and enliven his day. Not far from our home was an intersection which had a circular plot of grass in the center; cars were supposed to go halfway around the circle, then continue on in a straight line. It was this route I chose, hoping that for once, there would be no traffic. Speeding up to nearly fifty and noting the white car was still with me, though a little behind, I decided I was ready.

The intersection was coming up fast, Miraculously, no other cars in sight. My brakes squealed as the car completed the half-turn, squealed some more as it continued all the way around the circle. I had done it! Now facing my pursuer, I lifted a hand in greeting as I flashed by in the opposite direction. His deflated expression was worth my screaming tires, and I continued on my way, unhampered, to complete the secret mission of buying groceries.

Laughter was precious during the campaign, and the Burns Blitzers were about to provide some for the Rumpled Retinue.

The Blitzers were a team of formally organized supporters who traveled around the state by auto caravan in behalf of their candidate, Haydon Burns. Some were working men who used their weekends or took time off to campaign for the Governor; but Bob and Scott Kelly charged that far more were city employees of Jacksonville, notably big, burly policemen. The Governor denied this charge; the known policemen claimed to be on leave. But according to a friend in the Department, police radios were used in Blitzer motorcades.

Because their tactics were notorious, Bob occasionally began his speeches with, "Are there any Jacksonville policemen in the crowd?" The audience would laugh and wink knowingly.

The Rumpled Retinue, still on the lookout for a change of pace, created another game for mid-air play. It was called, naturally, "Blitzer," and went something like this:

Reporter, in megaphone yell: "Blitzer number one!"

Blitzer No. 1: "Hey-High! Tell 'em about the horsemeat!"

Reporter, same yell: "Blitzer number two!"

Blitzer No. 2: "How much did Bobby Kennedy put in your campaign?"

One of Bob's favorite sports, the climax to the Blitzer game was at hand. One morning Governor Burns again denied that city personnel were traveling as Blitzers. That same night the evening papers carried a story about a Jacksonville policeman who was arrested in Naples, Florida, along with a city building inspector from Jacksonville. They were charged with running a Burns sound truck without a permit.

This was too much for the Poet Laureate to resist, and the next day, the plane reverberated with a new song, to the tune of "McNamara's Band."

"Oh, me name is Al O'Reilly
And from Jacksonville I came,
To be in Haydon's Blitzers
And to advertise his name.
But when I walked along the street
A sergeant pulled his rank,
He said, 'There's Al O'Reilly
And he tossed me in the tank!
Oh, the music soars and the sound truck roars
But all to no avail,
For me name is Al O'Reilly
And I'm in the Naples jail!'"

Jacksonville, in addition to being home for the Blitzers, was the toughest city in the state for Bob. Yet it developed an intimate core of supporters who seemed determined to overcome the insurmountable. Those natives who were brave enough or foolhardy enough to declare themselves for High and work for his candidacy became accustomed to eggs splotched on their doorways, and their telephone being tapped; one couple returned home from a night's campaigning to find flames inching up a tree in their front yard, licking closer and closer to a High sign in the treetop.

The obstacles peculiar to Jacksonville acted as a stimulant. Some of the men met every morning at seven, rain or shine, at a downtown hotel, and a triumverate developed. Herman Terry, Don Bruce, and round-faced George Proctor.

"A Protestant, a Catholic, and a Jew," George quipped. "How's that for a threesome?"

One hectic day George rushed to the airport to meet Bob and his entourage, carrying with him sixty hurriedly-prepared sandwiches; he knew there would not be time for lunch, but at least everyone could eat in the cars, on their way to a meeting. The plane arrived half an hour late, and poor George was nearly trampled in the rush to the autos.

He shouted, "But look—here are sandwiches!" Nobody was listening.

"There I was, stuck with all those soggy sandwiches," he said. "So I started eating!"

Later that same day, Bob spoke before the Lions Club. The

Lions roared at George's one-sentence introduction of Bob.

"This is the first time in history that a Jew has introduced a Baptist to a bunch of heathens!"

Ten days before the primary, Bob sent Gene LeBeuf on a quick trip around the state to visit county managers. The campaign's fast and changing pace, the normal amount of confusion, made telephoning unreliable. Accordingly, Gene conducted a personal poll, beginning at the northwest tip of Florida and crisscrossing from one area to another.

He reported back, "You're in good shape, Bob. But Scott Kelly is coming on strong."

Ten days and Kelly coming on strong. Bob had nosed him out in a photo-finish to make the run-off in 1964. He wondered now if history would repeat itself or if the incumbent Governor had enough power and popurity to win without a run-off. Bob was a complex mixture of emotions, one minute declaring he knew he was going to make it, and the next, edgy, concerned, unsure.

A late-night call from Herman Terry brought new worries. Herman had a tip from the friendly Jacksonville policeman: two hoodlums from Jacksonville were headed for Miami with an undisclosed purpose that had something to do with the campaign.

"Be careful, Bob," he warned.

Later, the men involved in the episode which followed told what a crazy coincidence it was. Pure luck, they said. Two of Bob's aides, hulky ex-football players, decided to stay late at the law office one night. There was no particular reason, just a "funny feeling."

Midnight passed. All the lights were out except for a small lamp in the office they occupied; they spoke quietly. A sudden noise.

"What was that?"

From somewhere down the hall came a muffled grating, like a doorknob being gently turned.

"The back exit!"

They snapped off the lamp, half-crawled to the door, and listened. Soft footsteps padded from the direction of the stairway exit, ten flights up. Whoever it was had had a long climb and was breathing heavily. And he was not alone. The footsteps continued toward the reception room.

The two crouching aides could remain quiet no longer and sprang out the door, flooding the reception room with light. Startled exclamations ripped the strange tableau. Two rough-looking men, the two hoods from Jacksonville, were poised with a third companion, a man with a camera slung over his shoulder. They finally admitted the obvious: the hoods were going to have their picture taken in the law office of Mayor Robert King High. It would have been damaging.

Later, Bob simply shook his head. One finally reaches a point when the unexpected becomes commonplace.

Pure luck they were there, the young men had said. Maybe.

Sidelights of a campaign. My friends and I, on our last trip before the Primary, pointing our car toward the Panhandle. Coming abreast of other cars with High bumper stickers, kinsmen for a flash. Cars pasted with opponents' stickers, two sets of strangers laughingly wave each other away. Friendly service station attendants, "I sure hope he wins!" Yet another, "I wouldn't vote for him for nothin':" handing him my credit card out the window, mild shock and embarassment show on his face.

Our pace was so fast, impressions were fleeting, and it was only later, in retrospect, that all the minuscule things the subconscious registers filled in the vacuum. Yet there were incidents so vivid or colorful they needed nothing more than pen and pencil to capture the high spots.

Two men in the Panhandle happily related their successes. Said one, "I just got the Mayor 200 votes in a little town nearby. And there's only 200 people in the place!"

"How did you do that?"

"Why-y, I just told 'em that when he was elected Governor, he'd get the son of one of the town's leading citizens out of prison!" I winced.

Said the other, "Boy, I fixed 'em last night!"

I was almost afraid to ask how.

"I hired me a truck and a driver and we covered about fifty miles of highway, rippin' down all the signs of everybody but High! Didn't get back till almost four in the mornin' and dead tired! You just look, little lady, when you go on the next fifty miles. You won't see nothin' but your husband's name!"

I think I must have groaned. We left them looking crestfallen, no doubt plotting some new "old politics."

In the town of Milton, our host was a respected judge, a tall, rangy gentleman with a thatch of white hair; his lined face would have tempted any artist, and his voice was as Southern as corn whiskey.

"Am I goin' too fast for you?" he asked, his long legs covering sidewalk at a gentle lope.

"Oh, no," I panted.

We were walking around the town square. It was dominated, as are many small towns, by the courthouse; we had toured it, then a bank across the street. "A Kelly bank," the Judge said, for its officers were supporters of Scott Kelly.

"Are you too tired to go one more place?" He looked at me with a twinkle. "We can drive there."

"Fine."

"It's another bank," the Judge drawled, "a Burns bank this time. I'd just like to see the president's face when I bring in Mrs. Robert King High! Are you game?" The Judge suddenly looked like a small boy; he was irresistible.

He propelled me through the "Burns bank" with the grace of an old friend "just droppin' by." When we emerged, his old-world courtliness gave way to a howl of triumph.

"It was worth it. It was sure-ly worth it!"

We hoped Pensacola would be half as pleasant as Milton, unable to forget how it was for Bob two years before, on the steps of the Pensacola courthouse; and after a day of receptions and an evening of fish and hushpuppies, it was apparent Pensacola was a changed city.

The long day was nearing completion, and Sally and I rode with our Pensacola hosts back to our motel; Jenny and Dottie, driving my car, would meet us there for coffee. The county manager suddenly remembered the "High for Governor" billboard they'd wanted us to see; it hadn't been easy financing the billboard, and they were proud of it.

As he slowed down for an approaching red light, he said, I'll turn here, and we'll swing by for a minute."

The incident that followed was minor, but Dottie and Jenny

could not know it. Their story, as they told it later, left them shaken. They were waiting for us at the motel, and five minutes stretched into thirty. They began to fidget.

"You know, Dottie, that accident we passed," Jenny said. "For a minute I thought it looked like the car Faith and Sally were in. But then I told myself it couldn't be."

Dottie lit another cigarette. Twenty minutes more passed, and suddenly the phone rang; they both jumped for it, but Jenny got there first.

"Who is it? " Dottie mouthed.

Jenny held up a hand, then her hand began to shake. "Oh, no! Where? " A pause. "We'll be right there."

Dottie didn't need to ask, but she did anyway. "They've been in an accident." It came out a statement.

"F-Faith and S-Sally were both hurt, but he said not to worry, they were all right." Jenny started to cry, "I don't believe him, his voice sounded so scared."

They asked directions to the hospital, and Dottie drove while Jenny explained what happened.

"A drunk hit them from behind. The car was knocked through an intersection. Sally and Faith were both sitting in the back."

They got lost, stopped for directions a second time, then a third. Dottie was crying now. Finally the hospital appeared.

As Dottie parked the car, she asked, "Where did he say to go? "

"The emergency room." They ran as fast as their high heels would allow.

I looked up from the hospital bed into the weeping faces of Dottie and Jenny and decided the doctor had lied.

"Oh-h your face! " Jenny cried.

"What's wrong with my face? "

"Nothing! But I was afraid it would be all cut up! "

"You both look all right," wailed Dottie.

"You sound disappointed," said Sally, from the next bed.

A flustered nurse pressed Dottie into answering calls from the press, and she dashed in and out with dramatic reports. "The Police Deparmtent has had more than 500 calls! " "The Associated Press called! " "I just spoke with UPI! " She'd never be the same, we laughed.

Sally and I were released within the hour, and a frantic call from Bob, in Daytona Beach, came through. I assured him we were all right, and he was finally convinced when I said, "Would you believe the lengths I go to to get publicity for your campaign?"

An aide overheard the remark. "Ha! I'll bet the other candidates push their wives in front of a car tomorrow!"

On the way home the next morning, we remembered. We never did get to see the billboard.

Four days before the May 3rd Primary, Bob and Scott Kelly found themselves in vehement agreement. Bob was at a Miami television station to tape a nine-minute talk. The station had previously arranged for each of the gubernatorial candidates to record a speech; the tapes would then be spliced together and shown as a unit the night before the election. "Mayor High," the station manager said, as Bob snapped the microphone around his neck, "do you want to exclude the press from the taping?"

Bob thought it an odd question. "When is the Governor cutting his tape?"

"Not until Saturday." Saturday was two days away.

"What?" Bob exploded. "What's going on here?" That means I either have to tell the press not to cover me, or give the Governor two days' advance notice on what I say. This is another muscle tactic! Does he have that much power over this station?"

At that moment Scott Kelly walked in to prepare for his nine-minute tape. Bob quickly explained the situation to him.

"The reporters have a right to cover me, that's freedom of the press! This puts me in a position of asking them not to report something, and I've never operated that way."

Members of the press were crowded around, nodding in agreement. Kelly sided with Bob, and the two went off in a corner.

Bob and Scott Kelly, though near opposing ends of the political spectrum, had long maintained a cordial friendship. They had what staff members called a "tacit understanding" in this campaign; the two were running against the incumbent Governor, and they would leave each other alone, issues permitting. Now, in a corner of the TV station, they discussed their predicament. If they taped their speeches and barred newsmen, the press became the scapegoat; on the other hand, if reporters covered their speeches, Burns would have a tremendous advantage.

Moments later, the two announced their decision: they would both broadcast their segments live on election eve night.

The station manager hastily scribbled "number one" and "number two" on scraps of paper and thrust them toward the candidates to determine the order of appearance. Bob drew number one.

Election eve arrived and with it, the telecast. Bob looked tired, yet strangely relaxed, and as I watched the program from home, it became apparent he was making every effort to state his position clearly, to explain himself as a man. He spoke slowly, almost gently.

Many familiar phrases floated across the airwaves. "A new mood in government. . . I want to be governor, but not if I have to wear false colors. . . the issue is integrity. . ., I will never betray your sacred trust, so help me God."

Bob came home just before midnight, completely drained. "How do you think it went, Honey?"

"It couldn't have been better. How do you feel?"

"Oh, I don't know." A deep sigh escaped his lips; it seemed to come from the floor of the ocean. "I just don't know. I've done the best I can." A pause. "How do you think it'll go tomorrow?"

"I think whatever is supposed to happen, will." Bob knew what I meant, but I added the words anyway. "If He wants you to win, you will. If He doesn't, then there must be a good reason."

I received a tired smile. We'll just have to wait and see, it said.

By election eve's last sigh, the local papers had a headline for everyone: BIG VOTE FORECAST IN MIAMI—MAYOR HIGH IS IN TUNE WITH THE PUBLIC—EXPERTS SAY BURNS WILL LEAD—UNDECIDED VOTE IS HIGH. The experts were forecasting Burns without a run-off. One reporter wrote, "If he (Bob) isn't speaking over the heads of most of his listeners, what a surprise Tuesday's results could produce. The silent vote could speak, and for High."

The tally of daily newspaper endorsements were: Burns, 22—High, 6—Kelly, 3. It seemed so little to show for a march into hell.

But the human animal is a funny creature. Sometimes he has to be caught in the dark before he realizes the light was there all the time, waiting to be turned on.

In the voting booth

CHAPTER NINE

A Real Cliff-Hanger

The voting booth curtains were closed. Olive draperies stopped midway to the floor, revealing two pairs of shoes: a man's—polished black leather, heavy soles planted firmly apart; and a boy's—scuffed sneakers, one crossed over the other, rubber-toeing the concrete floor. Low murmurs and the metallic click of the voting machine sifted through the curtain.

The fire station, one of several hundred voting precincts in Miami, had undergone a magic transformation during the night. Big red fire engines were shunted outside to make room for the rows of curtained booths and registration tables, not to mention the early morning voters.

Long lines were beginning to form, people anxious to get to work. Some of them—my kind of people—were glassy-eyed, not quite awake; the disgustingly bright-eyed carried folded newspapers under their arms, shifting impatiently from one foot to the other. All eyes centered on the booth which contained the man and the boy. New arrivals, warned by the presence of cameramen, craned their necks; smiles riffled their faces as the scrubby sneakers uncrossed, then assumed a stance duplicating the man's.

The curtains opened and a smattering of applause broke out; guiltily it died away, as persons remembered they were not supposed to "politic" or otherwise express an opinion near voting places. Bob emerged from the booth, grinning widely and clutching the hand of our son, who looked a little embarrassed by all the fuss. No one at the fire station needed to ask who got Bob High's vote.

Inside my booth, our oldest daughter received her first lesson in voting. As I checked and re-checked "5-C" I had the horrible feeling that I would somehow pull the wrong lever. But "5-C" made a satisfying click.

Bob and I exchanged glances. His look was indicative of the long day ahead, the Big Day, the longest day. We hurried to the car, for there was much to do, "and miles to go before I sleep."

Eight P.M. and the longest night of Bob's career began. The polls had been closed for an hour now, and though election night was black and clear and warm, I was shivering.

For a change Bob and I were alone, driving toward the downtown hotel where supporters waited to see what the mood of the voters had been this day.

"Just think, the suspense will be over soon! "

"Yeah. Few hours."

Our conversation came out in sporadic gulps, for when we were not wrapped up in our own thoughts, we were listening intently to the car radio and the early returns. Our emotions swung like a pendulum, reflecting the moods of the newscaster; with satisfaction he declared it looked as if Dade County was going to produce a whopping vote this year. We smiled. But when he wearily said there were no significant returns yet, our smiles became ghastly.

Some voters were still standing in after-work lines. At least they cared enough to be there, Bob commented. And the weather, that political barometer, was no deterrent; happily, today the weatherman had miscalculated. There had been few of the predicted showers and Bob's skin, like that of most redheads, offered proof of a day in the sun.

In a matter of hours, I thought, we would see if the tan leather notebook with its section marked "Advance Checklist of Things to be Done" (Be sure the Mayor sticks to the schedule... clear functions with State Headquarters... enough cars to transport the Mayor and his staff... furnish reporters with local Western Union telephone number and a detailed schedule of functions... have enough overnight reservations, if required) had any important gaps.

A Real Cliff-Hanger

Election day is many things to many individuals. For me, election day was leaving the Bandwagon (now a fixture on the local election scene) at noon, on doctor's and husband's orders. Traces of the Pensacola mishap had not yet disappeared, but lying down at home, I found sleep elusive. It was like carting an injured football player off the field when he didn't know whether his team was winning or losing!

For Bob, election day was "playing your strength," and that meant racing to cover enormous Dade County, his home base, for one last time. Unlike some politicians who used voting day to catch up on sleep or quiet their nerves with a round of golf, Bob always campaigned until the polls closed at seven. In his philosophy there was no such thing as a sure winner, and for him 1966 was all or nothing. As usual, he ran scared.

Running scared to Bob meant push, push, push. It meant riding the Bandwagon to shopping plazas, changing to an automobile and heading for a hundred polling places, shaking hand after hand. It meant periodic checks with the Voter Registration Office in the courthouse to see how many were voting, watching the faces of strangers on the street, trying to decide whether they liked him, and if they did, was it enough to go and vote for him? Election day meant encouraging volunteers who stood under the beating sun with a High sign, saying it wouldn't be long now, yelling out, "I think the people are on fire! " It meant running, running, running; Scared.

When we arrived the hotel was a scene of bedlam—hot lights—rushing, sweating aides—voices and radios and TV sets. Months of work and planning finally showed in the faces of workers, and the strain of waiting for the votes to come in added lines and shadows.

Bob and I neglected our suite upstairs, because he wanted to be with "his people" on the floor of the ballroom. Hanging on one wall was a huge blackboard, a tote board, with a column for each of Florida's sixty-seven counties. Young ladies rushed back and forth, clutching pieces of paper and chalking in the mounting figures. The numbers changed fast, but their results were constant; as predicted by the experts, Governor Burns was leading. Bob and Scott Kelly were running close, first one out in front, then the other. It looked like a re-run of 1964.

Don Petit, tie loosened, shirt sleeves rolled up, looked the part of campaign manager. He was seated at a long table in front of a dozen telephones, asking the same question, over and over, of a hundred precinct workers.

"Where the devil is the Dade County vote? "

We wondered the same thing. Bob was counting heavily on his home county. It had to turn out for him, and turn out big.

"What do you think, Don? We're going to be in the run-off, aren't we? " Bob asked.

"Sure we are! Don't worry, we'll make it! "

Bob got on the telephones, talking to chairmen in key areas around the state.

"How does it look in Hillsborough? " His quick, relieved smile was answer. Then, replying to a TV station in Orlando, "Of course we're going to make it! We'll be in the run-off, all right! " His tone was almost a challenge, but his eyes could not hide the big question in his mind. Why wasn't the Dade vote coming in?

The wire services, the television channels, the radio stations, all were speculating on Big Dade's vote, wherever it was. "Rumors of a big turnout in Dade County may be unfounded," reported an out-of-town station. "We are not getting good tallies from there, reporting seems to be inaccurate. A state of confusion would best describe the scene at the Dade courthouse, where we are getting our figures. Or perhaps I should say," the announcer joked, "where we are not getting our figures. It could be that the little Mayor of Miami is in trouble! "

Bob disliked the situation, but he cared less for the newscaster's pessimism. "Get Jacksonville on the phone," he ordered. "Maybe we can find out what's going on there! "

Over long distance lines, a supporter described a relatively calm scene. Thirty men and women were munching on home-made cookies, drinking coffee, and listening to the wavering vote count on television.

"Just look at that! " George Proctor was disgusted, watching a telecast of the Burns headquarters where a victory celebration was in full swing with band and laughing crowd. The Burns organization had rented the huge Coliseum for the night, equipping it with a network of telephones and workers to handle reports from pol-

A Real Cliff-Hanger

ling places around the state; the installation could have done justice to a Presidential campaign. George munched his cookie defensively.

"Gloria, look at that!" he repeated. But George's wife was oblivious to him, to all the others in the room. She sat in front of one of the two TV sets like a robot, softly repeating, "He's going to win, he's going to win," fingers crossed, hands clasped in front of her, almost in an attitude of prayer.

Herman talked with Bob, saying that Jacksonville TV was reporting a shuttle between Burns and Kelly for the lead; Bob was now in third place. Miami was indeed lagging in its figures, and they wondered why. Then Herman had an idea.

There had to be an explanation for Jacksonville's advanced tallies, so he called a friend at the Burns headquarters. His friend confirmed the reason: the Burns organization, with its elaborate system and poll-watchers in every part of the state, was getting the vote count first and fastest—and the television station in Jacksonville got its information from the Burns headquarters! Herman's friend agreed to keep him, as well as the TV station, informed on the latest returns, so by this circuitous route the High headquarters in Miami was kept up-to-date by the Burns headquarters in Jacksonville. It was a switch.

By now TV pictures in Jacksonville began to show a somewhat grimmer celebration at the Coliseum. The Governor's supporters, confident of a first primary victory, felt the first seed of fear at the rising totals of Scott Kelly. Every now and then Kelly would jump ahead of Burns, then back to the second spot. But close, too close.

The Kelly people, sensing victory, sent a delegation to talk with Herman at the High headquarters. "We've got it locked up," they said. "We'd like to ask for your help in the run-off."

At that moment, a face familiar to those who followed political roads in Jacksonville appeared on the TV. It was Ed, Jacksonville's one-of-a-kind High supporter, and he was saying, "If we lose, we go to Kelly!"

Herman and George exchanged glances of surprise, dismay, anger, and humor. Ed had done it again! They turned to the Kelly men and told them the race wasn't over yet, they would wait and see.

On Herman's next call to Bob, he asked the question that was beginning to sound like an ominous drumbeat. "Where is the Miami vote? "

The polls in Miami had been closed for nearly four hours, and still Big Dade was yet to be heard from. Dade's ballot was absurdly long with sixty-nine different races and some two hundred candidates the voters had to wade through, but even the size of the ballot wasn't excuse enough for such a delay. The reason finally flashed through the tense High headquarters: the electronic machines which aid in counting the votes had suffered a nervous breakdown. While the monsters with the squiggly lights and buttons were being calmed and soothed by technicians ("Feeding 'em intravenously," someone said), the crowds that chain-smoked, consumed coffee, and assured themselves that High would make it, milled nervously and kept an eye on the tote board.

Contemplating the packed hotel ballroom, I was struck by a distinct contrast among the people, almost a self-devisiveness. A political campaign draws roughly three groups of people, and after a while the personalities become so basic, however varied, as to put themselves, almost mechanically, into one of three categories: People, Press, and Politicos.

The People are the "good guys" of the saga, idealists often, with enough realism to make them believable. They are the ones who cannot be bought, who would be shocked at the idea; the ones who have no special favors or privileges to curry, who are in a campaign, perhaps for the first time in their lives, simply because they believe in a candidate or what he stands for or both. Usually both. The People, no matter from what part of town they come, care about the dignity of man.

The Press, the ones who write and talk and photograph "color," add their own pallette of hues, in varying intensity. They are perhaps the most genuine articles to be seen in a campaign. Most are objective, standing in a corner, quietly but intently observing, drawing time-honored conclusions. The old-time news buff with press card sticking out of his hat is a thing of the past, but inside he has not changed. "The facts, man. The facts."

The last broad category of campaigners, the Politicos, are not the professional politicians—the candidates themselves—but rather

Mayor High in his campaign headquarters

the ones who merge quietly or noisily into the body of a campaign. The politicos cover such a wide spectrum they can be subdivided by recalling a sign that advertises a Florida tourist attraction: "Wierd reptiles, strange animals, and exotic birds."

The Reptiles are easy to spot. They slither along, ingratiating themselves with anyone they feel has power—whatever their definition of power, and they hold the belief that the end justifies the means. These are the dangerous ones.

The Strange Animals often do not make their presence known right away and are therefore more difficult to detect. They travel closely with the Reptiles, have many of the same characteristics, but they operate on a more subtle level. After all, the Strange Animals believe "one has to draw the line somewhere." It is a shaky line.

The Exotic Birds are not particularly dangerous, but they do have to be watched. These are perhaps the funniest and most colorful of the species, and therefore easy to detect. The Exotic Birds preen their feathers, pressing lapels, and grabbing ears with tales of their political acumen, how close they are to the candidate, and the many important jobs they will have when "their boy" wins. Often they are the life of the party, laughing it up with friend and foe alike because of their assurance in their magnetic personalities. Yet because of this assurance, sometimes they are pathetic.

While they seemed as different as separate races of humanity, most of the members of the People, the Press, and the Politicos, divergent as they were, did have one thing in common: Bob High. And as two families are linked by marriage, so were they by their candidate. The result was that they developed deep bonds or merely tolerated or couldn't stand one another, but they worked side by side anyway. Perhaps the unique feature of the High campaign was the candidate's unconscious power to make them want to help him.

Bob himself was a citizen of the world of politics. In spite of his homely background he was at ease with presidents, senators, ambassadors. Economic, religious, or ethnic differences went by the board, unnoticed; there was the vital catalyst of politics to dim the unimportant differences. Because of his background, and because he knew what made a man a man, he never lost Kipling's "common touch." In reality, he was something of a paradox, for he possessed the contradictory qualities of ambition and humility. The ambition to be in the center of things, to seek a position of leadership, and the humility to say, "I will try for it."

This night my paradoxical husband was experiencing every emotion known to politicians: hope, fear, pride, fear, confidence, fear. Scott Kelly was now 30,000 votes ahead of Bob, and Governor Burns was hanging on to the lead. Bob pinned his hopes on his home county.

"I figure Dade will come through with about 55% of the vote for me, and that'll put me in the run-off.

"It's going to go right down to the wire," he said, wiping a handkerchief across his forehead. "Right down to the wire! "

All at once he was ready to chew nails. The object of his anger was a local TV newscast composed of an IBM vote-projection machine and two political experts who sat in panel-formation and interpreted their machine's calculations. With authoritative insight, they stated, "It will be Burns and Kelly in the run-off."

The program's moderator reached Bob on a telephone-video hook-up, and Bob could not resist a sarcastic needle, reminding the newscaster that once before the station's IBM machine had goofed. He hadn't believed it then, and he wouldn't believe it now—until the votes were in.

"I can tell you one thing, my friend," he half-snapped, half-chuckled. "It's going to be a real cliff-hanger! "

Supporters standing nearby cheered and shouted their approval, while Bob whispered to me, through gritted teeth, How could those so-and-sos do that to me again?

"The prophets of doom," he growled, and turning to the crowd, shouted, "They counted us out once before! Just hang on, we'll make it! " I noticed half a dozen slip quietly out the door, but the remaining hundreds roared with one voice.

One who laughingly waved a clenched fist in the air was Daddy High, his blue eyes matching his son's, even down to the twinkle. He too was reliving a drama, one which took place in 1964 and ended in a victorious loss. Like his son, he had driven himself mercilessly, and like his son again, he repeated the process two years later.

On a recent trip he was driven 100 miles to the airport, missed the plane, and had to spend the night; next day he had to fly all over Florida, detouring to New Orleans, before he could get to Panama City, his original destination. This time wasn't wasted because one of his seat companions, a Florida resident, was converted to becoming a High worker in less than an hour! Daddy High's flying days ended after a trip over central Florida when the pilot tried to stay under a raging storm, instead of over it. In a matter of seconds they dropped a thousand feet, and after that, Daddy High changed to cars. He chuckled, "We were always on time, in the cars! "

Driven by a retired Judge, he covered every town in north Florida, chatting on the courthouse steps, drinking an icy coke in country stores, proving to all who met him, by his very countenance, that his son was no three-headed monster from Sin City. Standing before a microphone at a rally or a fish fry, he talked to the people—no formal speeches for him. Once, during one of these 'talks,' he paused a moment. The crowd began to applaud.

"I didn't aim for you to do that," he said, startled. "I was just tryin' to think of something else to say! "

On one trip to Jacksonville, where it seemed all roads led, I ran into Daddy High. "So, we meet again! Where do you go from here? "

"We-l-l, I don't know," he replied. "I reckon I'm like the old lady who was dyin' and her preacher asked her whether she was goin' to Heaven or hell. She said she wasn't sure, all she knew was she changed trains in Jacksonville! "

On this tense night his face hid nothing. His expression reminded me that in many High headquarters across the state was a Bible, opened to a particular verse someone had turned to while thinking about Bob's campaign. The coincidence of the verse, Romans 13:11, spread rapidly by word-of-mouth. "And that, knowing the time, that now *it is high time* to awake out of sleep."

A thumping head from my Pensacola accident, compounded no doubt by tension, sent me home shortly after midnight. I was now in bed, TV in front of me, transistor radio to the side. The vote count remained unchanged.

A Real Cliff-Hanger

The house was quiet and sleeping, but when I looked in his room, Bobby had stirred, mumbling, "Did Dad win?" I told him it wasn't over yet, we'd probably have to wait until morning to find out. I did not add things looked bleak.

I had left a gallantly optimistic Bob staring at the figures on the tote board. Some Dade County votes were beginning to trickle in, but not enough to make a difference. It was that time of election night when a few workers cried quietly into soggy handkerchiefs, when worry lines deepened in the faces of some, and the rest sat limply, ghosts of themselves. Only Bob remained constant.

"I've said it was going to be a cliff-hanger, and it is. But it's still not over."

I felt myself close up inside at his remark. My emotions agreed with him, that it couldn't be over yet, but logic told me it was. It would be different this time, I had thought, but now I wondered if I had talked myself into believing what I wanted to believe, falling into that too-easy trap.

I was paying scant attention to the TV from bed. Tired thoughts possessed by mind. It's all over... he wanted it so much.. worked so hard... should have stayed.. shouldn't have left him... I'm tired, so tired.

Like a bullet, a funny noise from the transistor burst in on my thoughts. What kind of sound was that? Why, it was coming from the newscaster! A gurgling thing, combined with a choked yell.

"Ha, ha! Lord Almighty!" he screamed into the microphone. "Listen to this!" And he rattled off the latest returns from Dade County.

"The little Mayor was right when he said don't count him out yet! Miami's votes are starting to pile in, and they're all going under the High column!"

The announcer, suave, cool, and sophisticated moments before, was beside himself; he was practically babbling into the microphone. I didn't know who he was, but I loved him.

"Here's some more," and he yelled out a new and rising total for Bob, sounding like a high school cheerleader. "Ladies and gentlemen, if you've gone to bed thinking it was all over, turn your radios back on!" He was nearly incoherent. "Because it's not over by a long shot! I think we're going to see history in the making tonight—or rather, this morning. I think a drama is unfolding before our very eyes. If you want to know what I think," and surely, by now, everyone in the radio audience did, "I think our Mayor, Bob High, is pulling a come-from-behind cliff hanger out of the bag!

"I've just been handed a new set of totals, and Bob is closing the gap between him and Scott Kelly. They're only eight, nine—yes, I think it's about nine thousand votes apart, and half of Dade County still to come in! Miami is witnessing history in the making! "

My headache gone, tiredness vanished, I was dressing again, rapidly. I had to get back downtown. The phone rang.

"Hello, Baby."

"Bob? Bob! I heard, I heard! " I was as incoherent as the newscaster.

"Get your clothes on, Baby, and come back down here! I'll send Ernie for you." His voice held a secret thrill, almost a passion. I nodded in agreement, as if he could see me.

It was anti-climactic. The longest day, the longest night, ended at 2:50 in the morning.

"On May 24th," Bob told the drained remnants of supporters who had hung on with him," I will be the Democratic nominee for Governor."

The People, the Press, and the Politicos still had enough strength left in them to cheer. The People clutched their ideals to their hearts, remembering how long they had believed; the Press wrote, "Nobody liked him. Nobody but the people." And the Politicos nudged one another, wisely nodding their heads; they knew all along "their boy" would do it.

The tote board reflected the final vote that put Bob in the run-off: Burns, 372,451; High 338,281. It was a cliff hanger in the finest tradition, for Bob inched ahead of Kelly by less than 7,000 votes. His strength was where it counted the most, where he and Petit had aimed their strategy: the populous counties, including Big Dade. He had played his strength for all it was worth.

The *Miami News* called it a "remarkable achievement... with little more than courage and the ability to win the confidence of a restless public."

In Jacksonville Governor Burns gave notice that in the second primary he would be "free to become Haydon Burns, the Candidate, call a spade a spade." He added he was "taking off the kid gloves."

Then the Governor turned to Scott Kelly and his 331,000 votes. "I have high regard for Mr. Kelly. He ran a good campaign, and the vote he received was a splendid tribute to him."

Those Kelly votes had to go somewhere, and the next big question to pound across the state was, whom, if anyone, will Kelly support? For the moment, State Senator Scott Kelly remained silent.

The second primary and the distribution of those 331,000 votes were only three weeks away.

CHAPTER TEN

The Big Push

Gene LeBeuf paced back and forth in front of the hangar, glancing at his watch every few minutes. The plane was nearly half an hour late. Gene could never hide his emotions, and this morning his impatience showed just as his anger had in Jacksonville with the qualifying night telecast.

He had fought the eight o'clock traffic to reach the private airstrip near Miami International on time; he could have slept another forty-five minutes, he thought. Or forty-five years. He needed it, but so did everyone else in the High campaign. And Bob? He wondered if Bob ever slept.

Where was the plane? Not only did his impatience show, but excitement as well. Jumbled together were his thoughts about Bob's potential defeat of the powerful Governor and the events of the past couple of days. Finally, those events took precedence, and his mind went back over them, step by step.

He knew about Bud's visit to Scott Kelly, the night before the election. What happens if Bob makes the run-off and you do not, Bob's law partner had asked. Can we count on your support? Kelly was in no mood to answer that particular question. Understandable.

But the follow-up was a switch, and Gene chuckled. On election night, when Kelly pulled ahead, some of his men came to High headquarters with the same question. What about Bob's support for Kelly? Wait a while, they were told; give the Dade County vote a chance.

The Big Push

Then Big Dade came in, and it was all over for Kelly. When the '64 Governor's race ended, Scott Kelly said, "I sorta feel like the game between Burns and Kelly was rained out. I feel like some day we'll replay it." His words were prophetic.

The next day he sent a telegram to 300 workers: "Due to incomplete returns and absentee ballots, we have not conceded. Request you do not make a decision on committing support to other candidates until you hear from me. You will be hearing soon."

By that night it was apparent absentee votes would change nothing, and Kelly conceded. He and his 331,000 votes became the pivot and reporters queried, "Senator, are you going to throw your support to Burns or High? "

Kelly had no comment, and political writers gazed into their crystal balls. "Burns will win the big one and Kelly will throw in with Burns! " Or another, "Scott Kelly will stay out of it! "

Both Bob and the Governor called Kelly, asking for his support. He knew some of his workers were meeting with their groups, he told them, but not at his direction. As yet, he had not made up his mind what he was going to do.

That same Wednesday night, Bob met with several of Kelly's top advisers. They assessed voting returns, estimated High and Kelly strength in different areas of the state, and figured that at best, Bob would garner only a small percent of the conservative Kelly vote. By midnight, they still wondered what action, if any, Kelly would take; he had promised a decision the next day. . .

Gene pulled his thoughts back to the present; it was more exciting than the past he concluded. Only a handful of persons knew whom he was meeting, and he couldn't help smiling at the thought. He wished they'd hurry, though; word was sure to leak out if they didn't. Word always leaked out. He looked at the sky. No small planes, only the big jobs, zooming their smoke trails across a shiny blue ceiling.

Gene lighted a cigarette and chuckled. He was thinking about the airstrip manager, a Burns supporter. The man had been out of his mind with curiosity. Gene was hardly out of his car before the questions began.

"See by your car you're backin' High."

"That's right, my friend. Don't you want to trade that Burns poster for one of ours?"

"Nope." A pause. "Meetin' friends this morning?"

"Yeah. I'm meeting friends."

"Not comin' in from the north, are they?"

"Nope."

The man's eyes darted toward the Burns poster. It gave him courage. "Where they comin' in from?"

"Central Florida." This yo-yo is too much, Gene thought. But he couldn't wait to see his face when the plane arrived.

He looked at his watch again. Fifty minutes late! He hoped nothing had gone wrong. All of a sudden, the unmistakable drone of a small plane coming in for a landing! The sun bounced off a wing, blinding him momentarily, and then he saw it clearly. This was it! Boy, oh boy, what a day this is gonna be!

"This the one you been waitin' for?"

"It sure is!" Well, my nosy friend, he thought, you're in for a surprise.

He hurried out to the runway as the plane taxied, cut its engines, and a door swung open. Two men and two women emerged. One of the men, square-jawed, with the gait of an ex-football player, walked briskly over and stuck out his hand.

"Good morning! I'm Scott Kelly."

As Gene hurried the visitors to his car, he remembered the Burns supporter and glanced over his shoulder. He was standing near the runway, mouth open, and bug-eyed.

The day before, Thursday, Kelly made up his mind. He told Governor Burns he was not going to support him, but he did not expect to take an active part in the High campaign. To Bob, his statement was the same: he would support him, he did not expect to be active, and he was working on his statement of endorsement for release that night from Lakeland, his home.

Bob was grateful for his decision, but he had a favor to ask. Couldn't Scott make his announcement from Bob's home in Miami? He knew time was short, that Scott needed to prepare his statement, so couldn't he withhold the announcement until Friday and fly to Miami with it? He knew that was asking a lot, he said,

The Big Push

but he didn't need to tell him how much greater the effect would be. Scott agreed.

So with great secrecy, Scott Kelly, his wife, his finance chairman and his wife, were ushered from plane to car to our home on Friday morning.

"Scott." Bob grasped his arm, probed his face intently. "You don't know how much this means to me." His face, solemn, said, I know how you must feel; but for a twist of fate, this could be me. Kelly returned his look—they seemed to be reading each other's minds—then all at once they grinned and the spell was broken.

State Senator Scott Kelly described himself as "just home folks," but the gleam of ambition was in his manner. Prematurely gray, tanned, and with the spring of an athlete in his step, he looked the part of a businessman in a hurry, eager to get on with it.

"Congratulations, Faith," he said, as we shook hands. There was a mercurial flash of something, almost a pain, behind his smile.

Then, with the hilarity of men too long under tension, they sat down to plan their announcement to the press; so far, they had succeeded in keeping Scott's trip a secret and were going to make the most of it.

"Remember, Faith," Bob cautioned, "If any calls come, you know nothing!"

The ladies and I had barely begun our first cup of coffee, in what was to be an endless succession of cups, when the telephone rang. And rang and rang. Reporters knew, instinctively or otherwise, something was in the wind. As Gene had thought, word always leaked out.

"Mrs. High? The Mayor there?"

"Yes, but he's busy right now. May I have him call you back?"

Or another. "I hear Scott Kelly may be on his way over there. Your husband around?"

And again. "Faith? This is Bill Baggs. I'll bet the Mayor's busy!"

"Yes," I choked "he is. I'll have him call you back in a few minutes."

No one had asked what I was afraid they would, but I knew my luck was running out. "All right," I whispered fiercely to Bob, "what do you want me to say when someone asks if Scott is here? "

Bob smiled. "Gene! " he yelled. "Don't let Faith take any more calls! She can't lie! "

Noon came, lunch forgotten, and more supporters trickled in, anxious to be at the center of the drama. Word finally went out. A press conference at the Mayor's home. Two o'clock.

By one-thirty our home had reached what was beginning to be its normal state of madness. Television men grunted and strained their way up the steps with hundred-pound cameras; radio men tested their equipment with a "one... two... three"; newspaper reporters wandered around what must have been familiar surroundings to them by now. I had the odd feeling they were at home and I a guest.

Supporters from the High and Kelly organizations introduced themselves to one another in varying degrees of warmth, cordiality, or suspicion. Many of Bob's aides were jubilant over the addition to their ranks; some were hostile. Kelly knew that Burns ran an iron-tight ship, they said, therefore his own chances of staying in the political limelight were better with High. And besides, even though he and Burns shared conservatism, he could hardly be expected to say, "Aw, I didn't mean those things I said about the Governor. He's really a good kid! " So they mingled and laughed and eyed one another, while camera crews made ready for the press conference.

They juggled furniture for the benefit of the cameras; someone pushed the love seat away from its spot in front of the fireplace and into another room, motioned Bob and Scott to it. The juxtaposition would spout the headline, "THEY SAT ON A LOVE SEAT...."

A director motioned for quiet, and all traces of uneasiness between the two groups vanished as if by remote control. "It's almost like inauguration day! " one whispered. Bob and Scott sat on the love seat grinning, joking, and laughing, an emotional cover for the moment.

The director mouthed one word. "Now! "

Defeated candidate Scott Kelly looked into the glaring TV lights and announced he would support Robert King High in the

The Big Push

run-off. He spoke of better education and integrity in government.

"On these two issues," he said, "the Mayor and I have agreed. These issues are more important than the political ambitions of any one man because they affect the lives of every human being living in the state of Florida."

The intense faces of the onlookers, men who knew the campaign trails inside and out, held a never-before and never-again look. Their eyes were bright.

Bob summed up their feelings. "What we have seen this afternoon is political history for the state of Florida."

Camera lights snapped off, reporters and aides began slapping the two ambitious young men on the back, guffaws abounded. Until a newsman from one of the wire services rushed up.

"Senator Kelly, have you seen this? " He thrust a paper out.

Governor Burns, meeting at that moment with supporters at a luncheon on Miami Beach, had charged that defeated candidate Scott Kelly offered, through another party, to sell his support to Burns for half a million dollars. Kelly's finance chairman, Ben Hill Griffen, was supposed to be the "bag man."

Scott laughed, handing the report back. "You've gotta have this mixed up! Not even 'ole Haydon would resort to such tomfoolishness! "

The wire service man looked puzzled. No, there was no mistake. Didn't the Senator have a comment?

An aide interrupted, carrying the pink sheet of the *Miami News*, the early edition. Its headlines blared the Governor's charge. There was no mistake.

Burns had taken his kid gloves off as he said he would, repeating that Robert Kennedy and the integrity of Bob High were the major issues. "If you want to talk about integrity," he said, "ask Mayor High how much it cost to get the endorsement of Scott Kelly. I wouldn't pay five cents."

Bob and Kelly stared at the report, for a moment with disbelief. Then Kelly saw red. "That's a damned lie! My God! "

He paced back and forth, his face got redder and redder. "I'll be damned if I'll take that! The Big Lie, that's what it is! Bob! I told you I didn't think I'd be active in your campaign—well, this tears it! I'll stump the state for you! You can print that! " he yelled at surrounding newsmen. "And you can call it what it is—The Big Lie! "

He called his Lakeland headquarters, told his people to start rounding up his supporters; he wanted them on the telephones. "Start sending out night letters," he barked. "I'm calling a meeting of Kelly people in Lakeland at two o'clock tomorrow! "

Kelly took Bob to the meeting with him. He talked about the Big Lie and told them he wasn't going to take it; would his supporters help him? He was going to stump for Bob High as hard as he'd stumped for himself. He was asking them to do the same thing.

They roared their answer. "Go get 'em, Red!" they shouted at Bob.

Tuesday, May tenth, two weeks before the run-off, and more than 250 persons stood in chilly, blustery weather at the airport in Gainesville, home of the University of Florida. Candidate High was having his usual plane failures and arrived an hour late; half-frozen supporters cheered, then hopped into their cars to form a motorcade. The caravan's length, over a mile, signalled an important event for this college town.

It was the Kick-off for Bob's second primary campaign, and he was to deliver a major address at the University of Florida. The locale was no accident. Bob had chosen the University town with care, for it represented quality education, one of the main issues in his campaign.

College students turned out in droves. Bob had a rapport with the young; often he seemed to speak to them alone as he asked them to share a new mood in politics. They had taken him literally today, for as the motorcade wound its way toward the college, enthusiastic boys and girls were everywhere, honking horns, waving arms frantically. The town was alive with signs proclaiming, "THIS IS HIGH COUNTRY! "

The crush at the University auditorium was a standing-room-only crowd of 2,000, and Bob summarized his education program for them . "Florida university salaries lag $1500 behind salaries paid in comparable institutions elsewhere, and soon the disparity will be $2,000. This will cause an exodus of scholars to other states.

Election morning, 1966

"I will ask for emergency legislation to make faculty salaries fully competitive. The job is not easy. Nor will it be quick. But we must start."

They interrupted with long and sustained applause. He was speaking their language.

"Governor Burns is going about, trading on the old fears of race and sectionalism. But even prejudice cannot save him now.

"The second primary will be a requiem for Haydon Burns and the pork chop politics of this state," and his right arm chopped into the air. "And he knows it! That is why his behavior these past several days has been so tormented and shrill."

The fever, in audience and speaker alike, began to rise. "Floridians will no longer tolerate hogpen morality in politics! "

It was easy to believe the signs that said, THIS IS HIGH COUNTRY, for the audience let him know it.

A student summed up the afternoon. "It was better than the time the 'Gators whipped Alabama 17 to 14! "

With his speech at the University of Florida, Bob's second primary campaign was off the ground. But he was angry. The Governor still repeated his charge that Kelly was willing to sell out for $500,000.

The press responded. A Jacksonville newspaperman revealed that two weeks before the first primary election, Kelly told him he would support High if he did not make the run-off himself. The reporter also recalled the Governor's words of election night, "I have high regard for Mr. Kelly."

A *Miami News* editorial asked, if money had been (Kelly's) objective, what is he doing in the camp of a candidate who raised only $140,000 in the first primary campaign? " Burns raised a million dollars.

A furious Scott Kelly traveled with Bob in western Florida, "Kelly Kountry," he called it. He must have made the Governor wish he had never said a word, telling red-faced crowds that Burns had charged he would sell his soul for half a million dollars, and that his children had asked him what it meant.

"I have no decision but to fight," he yelled, "and that's what I'm doing! "

Within a few days, the Governor backed off. "I do not consider the offer as being from a reliable source," he said.

But something had already begun to happen, to take hold of the crowds that came to hear the Candidates, as the papers dubbed them. To Kelly they'd shout, "We're with you! " And to Bob, "Tell 'em, Tiger! "

A story filed by reporter Bill Barry in the *Miami News* described the mood in one town.

". . . Then they rode into a town called Perry. Kelly's people, waiting, told him he'd better ride on to the next town. They said the streets were lined with Burns' men—wearing their white hats, and their hard eyes and their folded arms. They're all likkered up,' his people told him, 'just fixin' for a fight. You'd better ride on.'

"Kelly's eyes did a little clicking thing and something happened to his mouth. And he said, 'Let's go.'

"They rode in and Kelly started talking. He pointed right at the Burns men in their white hats, the red clay streaked on their boots. He told them about the rattlesnake that spits his venom in every direction when you break his back. He told them about trying to explain the Big Lie to his younger kids. He shook his fist at the Burns men and asked whatever had happened to their sense of honor and fairness.

"He made the dust crawl on the necks of the Burns men. And one by one, the white hats came off."

There was no let-up on the Governor's accusations. His opponent, he said, had been a "foreign agent" for the government of Venezuela "when it was under Communist control."

The *St. Petersburg Times* answered: "The Truth: High's law firm represented the government of Venezuela when it was paying off creditors in Miami for a bankrupt Venezuelan airline. As three Latin American scholars with Florida's university system noted for publication May 14, Venezuela has never in its history been under Communist control."

Burns then charged that High had the help of a "paid bloc vote" to get into the run-off, and that "bloc voting could make High win." He said, "The (Negro) bloc voting practice showed up in virtually every race in all major counties."

Again, the *Times* refuted the charge. "The Truth: In Hillsborough County (Tampa), Burns himself got 46.8% of the Negro vote. In Miami, April 11, Burns predicted he would receive 90% of the Negro vote."

Accusations tumbled head over heels as state employees were told their jobs were in danger. Burns workers ran full-page newspaper ads in the Panhandle stating that if Robert King High was elected, state employees would be fired wholesale and replaced with High people.

The charge simply was not so, Bob replied. "Normally, I wouldn't even answer Burns' charges," he said, "because what the Governor says in the morning, he usually retracts in the afternoon! "

Kelly was not so gently disposed, shouting to an amused audience, "I'm telling you, the man doing the most to elect Bob High is Haydon Burns and his big mouth! I only hope he doesn't get lockjaw before election day! "

On the heels of the Big Lie, the *Tampa Tribune* ran figures based on the candidates' spending as of May ninth. Their research showed Burns had spent $2.19; Kelly, $1.40; High, 38 cents—per vote. A case of simple arithmetic for the voters, Bob sighed: surely they could see he didn't buy his votes, much less Kelly's support. To strengthen his position, he disclosed his income tax returns. "Let Burns match that," he muttered.

As the days rolled toward the run-off, they increased in bitterness. I was grateful most of our children were too little to read the newspapers and understand. Our son, however, was older and understood far better than Bob or I realized.

Bobby had spent the night with a friend, and together they composed a letter. He brought it home for me to approve and mail.

"Dear Governor Burns: Since you are unwilling to meet my father in an open TV debate, I wonder if you would be afraid to meet me.

"I am eleven years old, and I have a few questions that I would like to ask you about your state policies. Sincerely yours, Robert King High, Jr."

I still have the letter.

CHAPTER ELEVEN

Run With the Wind

The bombshell exploded on us. It was planned and executed with the precision of an assassin's bullet.

Sunday, May fifteenth, 3:34 P.M. The crowds at Miami International airport, busy with their own affairs, hardly noticed the man who got off a Washington jet. He was Adam Clayton Powell, a Harlem congressman, and he called a press conference for four o'clock. When reporters arrived at the airport, Congressman Powell told them he had jetted in to discuss a labor bill with Miami labor leaders.

Near the end of the press conference, a TV man asked the New York Congressman whom he was for in the Florida governor's race.

"If I were a Florida citizen, black or white," Powell replied, "I would be behind High."

Adam Clayton Powell never left the airport and never met with local labor officials. At 6:00 P.M. he quietly boarded a northbound jet.

That night I heard the story from Bob, and as he told it, an expression was on his face I had never seen before, a peculiar mixture of defeat and fury. Bob was in Miami that Sunday afternoon, too, at an afternoon rally-in-the-park, preparing to address a crowd of several hundred persons, predominately black.

An aide rushed up, and as he whispered to him, the color left Bob's face as if he had been sprayed with gray paint. "Maybe it's just a rumor," he said. But inside he knew it was true.

They checked with newsmen and received definite confirmation of Adam Clayton Powell's unwanted endorsement. Bob slowly made his way to the podium. Then he got mad.

"You know how I feel about Civil Rights," he told the dark, upturned faces. "But this man is a bad man. It was a put-up job if ever I've seen one! " Many of the heads, quiet, serious, nodded in agreement.

"I don't know him. I don't want his endorsement. I would hope that he will go back to wherever he came from and tend to his own business.

"Gutter tactics will ruin this state," he declared. "And believe me, I intend to get to the bottom of this! "

Bob got to the bottom of it, and he called a news conference to expose the results of his digging. The black attorney who had angled for appointment to the vacant City Commission seat became miffed when he was by-passed for Mrs. Range; he switched his allegiance from High to Burns. And he had spent the previous Thursday and Friday in Adam Clayton Powell's office.

The final piece of the jigsaw puzzle was the reporter who had asked Powell what he thought of the governor's race. Bob produced a letter from the TV station in question. It said the person "is not a member of the news staff. He was not assigned as a representative of this station in any capacity to cover Sunday's news conference." The plan had been a simple one; that was its grotesque beauty.

Scott Kelly, present at Bob's conference, revealed his own piece of information. "The opposition has planned to have a motorcade of blacks go through western Florida with Bob High's literature and stickers for no other purpose than to try to inflame the people of west Florida on racial matters."

Then a reporter asked the question that was torturing me. "How much more insanity is there going to be before this thing is over? "

At the end of the day, Bob High, candidate, became Bob High, man. But the vital spark was missing, his eyes were tormented. We tried to talk of other things, but our conversation kept turning back to Adam Clayton Powell.

Suddenly Bob grimaced and began rubbing his left arm. I knew the signs and, saying nothing, brought him a tiny, white pill. He put it under his tongue.

The grimace slowly vanished from Bob's face. The nitroglycerin pill, setting off its tiny explosion, had done its job. And the others, using their own brand of explosive, had done theirs.

"There has never been a campaign for the governorship in this state similar to the one being waged now," stated Bob.

The candidate and the ex-candidate were traveling together, unheard-of in state politics. From flatbed trucks on dusty roads to metropolitan centers to the comparative privacy of the airplane, one thing was obvious: they were enjoying themselves. Take away the dead seriousness, the heavy drama, and it was almost like a road show. The crowds who came to watch, even those who watched through narrowed eyes, were exposed to the developing camaraderie between the two. No sir, they'd never seen anything like it before.

At one stop, High delivered a "Kelly" speech, doing a take-off on him, shoving his jaw forward. And the people who had waited for nearly three hours roared with laughter. Bob looked up from the stage to see Kelly approaching. "Scott," he said, "I've been fooling around, having a little fun telling the people how we've been spreading the word. I just don't have another speech in me!"

And Kelly shouted, "I feel one COMIN' ON!"

The growing rapport between the two men and the people was apparent offstage. At the end of one particularly backbreaking day, red from the sun and weary from the pace, they were shuffling through an ancient hotel lobby. It was a little after midnight, and if they were lucky, they might get four or five hours' sleep before morning.

Suddenly Bob saw a familiar figure about to go out the door of the hotel. "You want to hear some barbershop?" he said to Scott. "Man, there's nothing better than barbershop. Come on!"

He grabbed Scott's arm, yanking him across the lobby after the Miami singer. The young man, member of a barbershop quartet, had attended a meeting of the Society for the Preservation and Encouragement of Barbershop Quarter Singing in America with his three harmonizing buddies; they quickly agreed to reassemble and "sing for our governor."

Word flashed among departing society members, and they began filtering back into the meeting room. Kelly was standing apart from Bob now, smiling at him fondly. Fatigue gone, Bob sat on a table, tapping his foot and nodding his head in rhythm with the music. The quartet wound up with "Hey, Look Me Over," and autographed a record jacket for the candidate. As Bob made his way upstairs, Kelly noted that his footsteps were no longer dragging.

Of course, the Bob and Scott show was not all harmony. Each new day brought a new insinuation, and when Bob was not the target, those surrounding him were. Riding the horse of demagoguery, the Governor was beginning to shock those not easily shocked.

He charged that a portly, grey-haired supporter of Bob's was a "known gambler" who promised $100,000 to the High campaign. By the next day, the Governor had promoted the gentleman to "one of the biggest gamblers in south Florida," and finally, "a prominent member of the gambling syndicate."

The object of Burns' accusations was a fair concession operator who also served on the Board of Directors of Variety Children's Hospital; he had contributed the legal limit of $1,000 to the High campaign. He had also been asked to support the Governor months before and refused.

Bob jockeyed from one angry situation to another, saying Burns was trying to assassinate the character of everyone opposing him. Reporters, noting that the urbane veneer was cracking, said Governor Burns had fallen prey to a common disease among politicians known as Foot-in-Mouth, and often fatal.

Next, Bob received a tip that the airplane he used would be sabotaged.

"Anything would be an improvement on these planes! " a reporter remarked.

Searchers found nothing more than a tape recorder, fastened underneath one of the seats, but after that the plane was never left unguarded.

The sabotage threat merely sent the Bob and Scott show to the skies in redoubled efforts. It had a curious effect on Bob because it made him angry; and anger seemed to sharpen his senses, to bring his thoughts together machine-gun fashion. It

Run With the Wind

made him become, as one reporter put it, coldly eloquent.

By now his chances were at least even. Analytical figures, if one trusted them, showed that he needed 57% of Kelly's 331,000 votes to win, and that Burns needed slightly more than 43%. In the '64 race the conservative Kelly vote would have been written off for Bob, but this time the campaign trail told a different story.

In northwest Florida, where moss hangs low on the trees and red clay announces that Georgia is not far away, the crowds got larger. The motorcades from airstrip to town and back again grew and grew until they looked like a gigantic snake weaving its way through the countryside; and from Pensacola to Tallahassee, the cheering got louder. Milton is where the cheering began.

The master of ceremonies, using words that never would have been used to describe Bob High in the Panhandle two years before, said, "It's been a long time since a governor visited us. We've got one here today. BOB HI-U-UH!"

"I believe as Thomas Jefferson believed," Bob said, "that a public official is public property. I believe in good, clean, honest government where your hard-earned tax dollar isn't thrown away to some political crony."

He was speaking to good, clean, honest people, talking from the back of a flatbed truck. The shade of the live oak trees along the road was not enough to keep the searing sun away from men and women who had taken time off from the fields or the kitchen. But the hot afternoon rays didn't seem to matter. Calloused hands were busy, clapping with a thunder that could be heard all the way to the capital.

"Cronyism is not my kind of government. I will not tolerate it. I will eliminate it. Businessmen don't have to crawl through a campaign with me to do business with the state." His voice grew louder. "I don't want to get agonized in office with things I can't do. I won't promise things I can't deliver!"

He talked about his beginnings on the farm in Flat Creek, Tennessee. He talked about the Depression and poverty and the war. He said, "Isn't it a wonder that I . . . the opportunities of America. . . ."

He tried to go on but could not. The right fist chopped into the left palm, and still he could not go on. He shook his head.

But the people understood. And the flatbed truck rocked with their cheers.

Seasoned and cynical observers of politics used words like "incredible" to describe his reception in the panhandle. And from there, like the rumble of an Indian drumbeat, the cheering moved east.

At a university, using an overturned garbage can for a lectern, he spoke to a mixed group of young and old. "Great moral changes are born in dreams of farm boys on hillsides." You knew by the brightness in his eyes it was a personal statement.

"I want to see that all young, future dreamers have the same opportunity.

"There is a revolution in this state. It is a revolution of character and conscience. I tell you," and he almost glared at the audience, so intense was his gaze, "this election is going to be won on moral tones rather than politics. I guarantee you that.

"I promise you this. If you and the people of this state send me to Tallahassee, never—*never*—will you be ashamed to say, 'This is my governor.' "

Like a low growl from the throat of the 'gator, a chant began. It said, "We want High! " and it grew to a roar that mixed with thunderous applause. The Indian drumbeat was still moving, and it turned south, rumbling down the Gold Coast like a giant wave.

The redhead was shouting to Kelly, shouting to be heard above the roar. "This has been the day! We've broken Haydon Burns' back! We're going to win! "

Friday, May 20th. Four more days to go. Another airport scene, this time in the hot spot. Jacksonville. In February there were twenty men working in the High organization there; now there were three hundred, and most of them seemed to be on the very spot I was standing, a white square of asphalt outside a cavernous hangar.

The usual impatience of those who always seemed to be waiting for High planes was missing. In its place was a kind of elation, for this was a big day in Jacksonville. For weeks organizers had carefully planned this day—a large motorcade into town, speeches across the street from city hall, more speeches in a park—and all was ready, waiting for the candidate. But I had a funny, nagging sensation that wouldn't go away.

"Herman, I surely hope everything goes well. I have the funniest feeling."

"Stop it, you witch! Everything's going to go fine!"

I hoped he was right. Jacksonville had had its share of things going sour; at the recent opening of Bob's new headquarters for the second primary, the lights mysteriously went off in the middle of the ceremonies.

Bob's plane was approaching, and people began heading for their cars; two policemen, escorts for the caravan, jumped on their motorcycles, adding a f-fr-ooom to the already noisy sound of automobiles, voices, and a whistle from the jet. This plane, looking like a graceful dove as it streaked toward the ground, was a 500 mile-per-hour Lear jet, a conversation piece in the High campaign because of its airworthiness.

I boarded the plane and surprised a dozing Bob. I should have been halfway to Miami by now, but my friends and I had delayed our departure so I could say hello and goodbye to my husband. His fellow travelers quietly eased out, leaving us alone for a minute. We had time for a "Hi" and "Are you all right?"

My friends and I said goodbye, wished everyone luck, and climbed into our car to head for Miami. We would be leaving before the motorcade got under way. To our surprise, the motorcycle policemen stopped all traffice and waved us onto the highway, and the next moment the officers signalled the caravan cars to fall in behind us. They thought we were leading the motorcade!

"No! No!" we called, frantically waving them back. "We're not in the motorcade! We're going to Miami!"

We were already on the highway, bottling up traffic, before the officers understood. One slapped his head, then motioned to a dozen High cars that had dutifully fallen in behind us, to back up.

I hoped this wasn't an indication of what would happen to Bob in Jacksonville. But I couldn't rid myself of the feeling that it was.

Among papers in the High organization was one entitled, "Motorcade Guideline." The Jacksonville group had met the requirements: two to four motorcycle policemen as escorts, schedules of the route to be taken for policemens' use, necessary permits already secured (for this day, they had been told by officials none were necessary), cars lined up before Mayor High's arrival, press cars placed behind the candidates's car. But something was going wrong.

By the time I reached Miami, several long distance calls were waiting to tell me what had happened. The motorcade got split in several parts, the motorcycle escorts made wrong turns, there was chaos at the rendezvous point. Someone announced the park rally had been mysteriously scratched; rumors flew that the Blitzers were at work.

A big bus, carrying food and more supporters, was angrily waved away by an officer. He told them they could not park in the lot without a permit.

"We applied for one," an aide explained, "but they told us we didn't need it! " The officer told them to move on or else.

In desperation, Bob hopped to the sidewalk and began shaking the hands of passers-by. But the caravan had to move on. As the candidate reentered the bus, a man wearing a Burns button sidled up. "How'd you like the way we messed up your parade? "

"We'll pull it out, yet," Bob said grimly. "We'll pull it out."

Farther on down the street, they spied a long line of persons waiting to buy license plates outside a tag agency, "getting ready to pay tribute," Bob said. In a flash he was on the sidewalk again, shaking more hands. Suddenly the line started to move forward, as if pulled into the tag agency by an invisible rope. The reporters scribbled furiously. They realized what was happening, and the columns they filed told the story.

Word came that the rally was on again. Industrious aides had scurried through the park, rounding up everyone who could walk.

From a makeshift podium Bob said, "We are going to make history in this state! We are going to take the government away from the iron fist and give it back to the people."

And the crowd said, "Amen! "

"Just the other day," Bob shouted, "Governor Burns said he had heard enough about integrity to last him a lifetime. I don't like to belabor a point, but he's going to hear a lot more about it before this campaign ends! "

Run With the Wind

They did manage to "pull it out." But the day's events in Jacksonville, unknown to them, poured fuel on an already blazing fire.

It was just after midnight when our telephone rang. I was tired and paid little attention until I heard Bob's startled exclamation.

"They did WHAT? " Silence. "Well, who is he? " And then, "Thanks for the information."

He immediately placed a call to Herman in Jacksonville, asking him to go out and buy a morning paper and call him back. He looked sick as he told me what happened.

Bob had used an open convertible for a portion of the frantic Jacksonville parade. At one stop, someone shoved a man into the convertible with him, saying, "You don't mind if one of your workers rides with you, do you Mayor? "

Bob said he did not mind, though he didn't know the man. He was pleasant and told Bob how he had been handing out brochures for him; he seemed pleased to be able to ride with the candidate. It was all innocent enough. But Bob did not know that his passenger had been set up as a patsy; his passenger didn't know it either.

According to Bob's informant, someone took a picture of the convertible and its occupants with a long-range camera, and the resulting picture was to be used in a paid political ad for the Jacksonville papers. The reason someone had gone to so much trouble was that Bob's passenger was out on parole from a felony.

Unbelievable, I thought. So much was unbelievable, like the ugly billboards we saw on the way out of Jacksonville, proclaiming, "Their candidate will win unless you vote—keep Burns governor." Racism. Frame-ups. A political form of insanity.

Herman called back within the hour. His news was bad. The ad was in the morning edition, running nearly half a page, and featured a picture of Bob, Scott Kelly, and another man riding together in the open convertible. The ad read:

"*A man is known by the company he keeps . . . Above: Robert King High and his Jacksonville motorcade companion, convicted criminal,——. Robert King High is shown with one of his associates in his Friday Jacksonville motorcade, none other than ——. —— pleaded guilty for his part in the insurance-car repairing scandal, . . . he was sentenced to serve 18 months in jail in Division A,*

Criminal Court by Judge William T. Harvey. These conspirators faked repairs on automobiles and were paid by the insurance company. Your insurance premiums paid for the entire episode.

"Robert King High and convicted felon — — ... are these the kind of buddies you want running Florida for the next four years? Keep Haydon Burns your All-Florida Governor. 'Paid Political Advertisement.' "

Bob waked the editor of the paper in the middle of the night, but the executive protested he did not handle "that sort of thing." Bob was furious. I was sitting on the bed, aghast; I thought I knew my husband well, but never before had I heard him use such a savage tone. I didn't much blame him. The editor decided, at the mention of the word lawsuit, to see what he could do, and the ad was pulled from the evening edition. But it was too late to stop the morning presses.

And the days and hours clicked by with renewed vengeance.

Another Sunday afternoon rally in Miami, with the run-off only two days away. This time the weatherman was uncooperative, and rain kept an expected overflow at the Miami Stadium to a few thousand. Nevertheless, the sights and sounds of a political rally filled the ball park. There was fried chicken, soda, and popcorn; a voice over the P. A. system described a lost five-year-old who wanted his daddy.

As we entered the stadium and made our way to the platform, the band was playing "Hello, Dolly." A shower of red, white, and blue balloons came cascading down, and the cheers were deafening. Bob was on his home grounds, and he loved every minute of it.

The master of ceremonies walked to the microphone. "INTEGRITY DAY IS TUESDAY! " he yelled. Cheers. Then he introduced Scott Kelly.

"Political history is being made," Kelly said. "Never again will a politician try to stir up racial prejudice to get elected to office. Racial prejudice in political campaigns will be dead! "

Yet even now, the Governor was urging everyone to go to the polls Tuesday to offset what he called "the paid Negro bloc vote."

Bob came to the microphone. "The people have been governed

Run With the Wind

by a political machine long enough!" he said. "Private citizens, whose only crime was taking an opposite stand in an election, have had their character assassinated. The people of Florida never have to be afraid of that kind of government any more. It's over!"

Character assassination was not the only form of persecution High supporters had suffered. One man, an executive in a citrus company, was told to stay out of the High campaign or his products would be discontinued by a large Florida grocery chain. The businessman stayed with High, and his product was pulled from the stores.

An officer in the same grocery chain issued an identical ultimatum to another High supporter, a grain producer. Like the first man, he stayed with the campaign; the next week, grocery shelves which once carried his corn meal displayed another brand.

"This is the first time," Bob continued, "that a candidate will be elected with little money or organization or other resources except..." and a pause, "except the strength of you and people all over the state.

"This is a great time to be a Floridian. There are things to do in this state—burdens to bear, challenges to meet, opportunity to welcome, great events to witness, hope to savor, and a future to dare!

"Let's be on with it!"

And the rain could not drown out the sound that came from 2,000 throats.

Election Eve. You run with the wind, refusing to let fear dog your footsteps. But you know that somewhere behind you is a shadowy Thing, and you try to cram as much as you can into one day, hoping to stay ahead of It.

Scott Kelly flew west, into his Kelly Kountry; Bob flew east, determined to cover the cities along the Gold Coast for one last time. He was to be in Miami that evening at seven for a TV taping, and at 8:30 P.M. he was due in Tampa, on the west coast, for another television slot.

"They're going to kill him," said a supporter.

Sometimes a campaign has what is known as a "last-ditch stand." This one did. Governor Burns cut a TV tape in Tallahassee, displaying the "convicted felon" ad and trying to link Bob with "outside forces" and "known gamblers and criminals."

Then he did a strange thing.

He dodged newsmen and jetted to Albany, Georgia, and Dothan, Alabama. He made a television tape in Albany and another in Dothan. Both stations reached northwest Florida; both tapes would be beamed into Florida living rooms that night; and both smacked of racism and the same tired charges.

A reporter who didn't give up easily traced the Governor's movements and called Bob. That night, after Bob's appearance in Tampa, he took a hair-raising jet ride to Panama City, where the program from Albany was being carried. The TV station in Panama City had previously refused Bob time on election eve, but after Burns' broadcast from Albany they capitulated, and station officials promised Bob equal time. Pilots pushed the jet to its structural limits, and it screamed into Panama City, where Bob jumped into a waiting car. Within minutes he was standing before TV cameras.

For the last time he replied to the Governor's charges. For the last time he tried to assure state employees that their jobs were not in danger.

"The outcome of this race is more than who will be governor," he said. "The outcome is the kind of state you'll have, not only for your generation, but for your children."

There could not have been much fight left in him as he wearily returned home at three in the morning. It had been over nineteen hours since his head last touched a pillow.

He smiled the shadow of a smile. That was still left, and a flicker of something else. The Thing had finally caught up with him. Fear.

You knew it was so, because the only words he spoke were, "I wonder if I did enough?"

CHAPTER TWELVE

The Magic City Explodes

"Hey, look him over, he's your kind of guy,
    First name is Bob
    His last name is High.
Candidate for Governor of our Sunshine State,
There's only one man who can fill the bill
    Between Key West and Jacksonville..."

The Bandwagon was on the move, the big truck rolling up and down the streets of Miami with its cargo of nomads for a day. All the members of the cast were there: the candidate and his wife, the ladies in their matching red, white, and blue outfits, straw-hatted Jimmy Peck and the band, and assorted extras—members of the press. On this run-off election day the Bandwagon had the elements of a television spectacular. Music, drama, comedy, mystery, color, and high suspense.

The music, a proven attention-getter, was mere background today; for when startled passersby recognized their Mayor, red-faced and clutching a microphone, they switched their absorption to him, staring, smiling, waving, calling out.

He asked the people to give him their hands and hearts, and by the way, their votes. "I feel I have to reach out and touch the people," he told a reporter. "My home county." There was happiness in his face, and nostalgia, as if he wanted to remember this day, these people, forever.

A fever burned in those who rode the truck, and wherever the

Bandwagon went, the fever spread. A teen-aged girl jerked her hand loose from her boyfriend and began waving frantically. "Mayor! Mayor High! " She was desperate that he see her and flushed prettily when he waved back; at an expressway construction site the band played the "Anvil Chorus" in perfect tempo with the pile driver, while laborers, high atop the unfinished bridge, doffed gleaming metal helmets; a young couple from England followed behind the truck for a while, and at a stop light they dashed from their car.

"This is the jolliest thing we've seen in the States! " they exclaimed.

The big truck rolled to a stop at the Robert King High Towers, a high-rise complex for the elderly, and at the sound of the music tenants streamed out of the building. For many of them the Bandwagon was a diversion; but it was more. It didn't take a sociology major to recognize that for these old people Mayor High was a symbol of their own passing youth and vigor; he had shown concern for them over the years, and they knew he cared; their faces reflected it.

One man, leaning heavily on a cane, cupped his free hand around his mouth and yelled, "Vote second degree Burns—vote High! " Bob threw back his head and roared.

As always on election day, the Bandwagon went to the place of its birth, our old neighborhood and Princess Park, renamed Robert King High Park. We passed our former home, and I had a vivid memory of the grey-panelled porch, a few friends seated around a circular table, late at night, talking, hitchhiking on one another's ideas, when suddenly, ecstatically, the Bandwagon was conceived. Nine years ago.

The fever reached its zenith in downtown Miami, an unlikely place. Shoppers, tourists, businessmen, busy people, normally unconcerned, became actors in a slow-motion reel. They saw Bob, recognized him, and began to smile and wave. not caring whether they were conspicuous or not; they leaned out of office windows; a group waiting for a bus started clapping. Workers came out of the Burns headquarters, arms folded. Slowly their arms unwound, and they exchanged salutes with the nomads on the truck, laughing self-consciously. It had never been quite like this before.

The Magic City Explodes

Even the reporters were caught up, waving, writing, and hanging on to the side of the truck at the same time. They didn't need to make up color today; they had to choose from the overabundance of it.

"It's like he's a hometown hero! " one said. "Is it always this wild? "

Bob was playing his strength, and today explained the meaning of the phrase. His strength was the people. And they sensed something, the same thing I had felt a few days before, with certainty. He was going to win.

Suite 1502, the Everglades Hotel. Huge plate glass windows, high above Biscayne Boulevard, looked out on black velvet studded with shimmering tinsel: Miami at night.

It was a far different city from the one Seminole Indians had named "Big Water" or "Sweet Water," when 'gators prowled across what would one day be the FEC railroad tracks, and when Chief Tigertail followed the trail from the swamplands to trade with the settlers. That was back in the 1890's, and now Miami was a young lady, barely old enough to vote, historically speaking. She still suffered growing pains and juvenile lapses, and at night she wore all her jewelry at the same time, appearing gaudy and overdressed, a bedeviled sorceress, and a lovely fairy princess all at once. She was bubbly in her youth, and because she had a heart big enough for everyone, she would soon come of age. And tonight, for better or for worse, she belonged to Bob High.

Bob was seated in front of a telephone, jotting down figures one minute, swiveling to catch a late return from TV the next. Or he was up, pacing with ill-concealed excitement, exchanging stories of the day with the small group of supporters gathered there. He laughed, he smiled a lot, the little boy grin of pure delight; but once in a while an unseen force drew him to the window, and he looked into the blackness and the lights as one might look at his beloved. The Magic City. She poured out her benediction on him today, tonight. His eyes were moist.

The votes came in fast; there was no delay as there had been three weeks ago, and Bob was steadily increasing his lead over Burns. The enthusiasm on the Bandwagon had been a harbinger, and Miamians ignored the afternoon rain to cast their ballots as if, sensing a victory for their Mayor, they wanted a tangible share in it. And a ballot is a tangible thing.

I had left the Bandwagon in time to go to the beauty salon, and driving home in a steady rain, I wondered about Bob and the girls and the band; they probably had to cut their tour short because of the messy weather.

Suddenly, from the radio: "This is Ralph Page, WGBS total information news, following the High Bandwagon." It had begun to rain, he said, and the candidate was riding in a car. "But the rain has not dampened the spirits of this campaign—nor of the five young ladies riding the back of the High Bandwagon, a huge, open truck! " Oh, no! "They are real troopers, literally singing in the rain! " Through gritted teeth, I thought.

After a repeat of our usual election night routine—a bite of dinner, frenzied dressing, reporters and aides clamoring for attention downstairs—Bob and I arrived at the Everglades Hotel.

An arrival, the pulling up of a car, the alighting of its occupants, is a commonplace thing. But not this one. It was phenomenal. We chose an obscure side entrance because of the crowds, and even it was jammed with people. Cars were double-parked, temporarily abandoned; two policemen vainly tried to clear a path; and finally, aided by a couple of bystanders with large shoulders, they did.

It looked as if everyone in the city had come downtown to share in what they knew was going to be a celebration. They jostled for a place on overworked elevators, heading for the rooftop ballroom where supporters had gathered to wait for returns. Bob and I went first to Suite 1502, and as our elevator door slid noislessly closed on the phalanx of party-goers, it became a steel curtain signaling the end of Act One.

Act Two was now in progress, and Bob decided to get in touch with the west coast and "see how they're doing over there."

The west coast had a problem similar to Miami's: too many people and not enough room. Bill Burmeister, the St. Petersburg chairman, asked himself where all these people were before, when he really needed them! He was outside the headquarters, standing on top of a car, the only place he could be seen and heard by the excited crowds, trying to announce the latest returns and tell them

The Magic City Explodes 155

their candidate was winning. It seemed they already knew. How different it was from the first primary, when they all cried, even the men, because they thought Bob was losing.

Inside the headquarters Bill Minteer, tall and rangy and sweating profusely from the heat of too many bodies, was thinking all the way back to the '64 campaign. He had seen a newspaper article that the Mayor of Miami was planning to run for Governor, discussed the story with his wife, and said that somehow this young mayor seemed for real.

Funny how word gets around. Though he wasn't a follower of politics, Bill was asked to work on the High campaign. Before he knew it, he was heading up a county!

Like many others, he found the High campaign was no bed of roses. The office, again like many others, had no bathroom. It became almost a mark of distinction to see which High headquarters had the least plumbing.

Bill would never forget a trip he made with Bob to Winter Haven. Their Piper Cub was running late as usual, flying through thick clouds. Bob was asleep, so Bill turned to the pilot.

"Have you flown much?"

"Nah! This is my first time."

"How does the weather look to you?"

"Didn't check the weather. Forgot, I guess."

There was a parade in Winter Haven, and mobile homes were set up on the fairgrounds for each of the six candidates. A man entered Bob's trailer, carrying a briefcase, and with a snap of the lock disclosed a mountain of bills.

"There's $10,000 in here," he said to Bob, "and it's yours for the campaign. If you win, I want to set up a race track in Volusia County."

"There are five other candidates and five other mobile homes here," Bob said, cutting him short. "Get out!"

Bill had to admit one thing. The airplanes this time were still broken-down. Only a couple of months ago he was flying with Bob when the lock on the door fell off, the door flew open, and all their papers were sucked out in a whoosh! to be scattered over the Glades. The birds and the 'coons got some political education, he guessed.

What a long road the High road had been, he thought. For all of them.

At ten minutes after nine o'clock in Suite 1502, a skyrocket suddenly burst. There were shouts from the men and a stifled sob from Bob's mother, who sat quietly on the sofa. A terse message had just flashed across the TV screen:

"Wire services nominate Mayor Robert King High."

The wire services, unlike the vote projection machines used on television, rarely made a mistake, and their seven word statement rolling across the screen opened the door of emotions, just a crack, for those who waited in the room. Bud Stack and Ned Davis, Bob's law partners, had urged Bob to wait until 1970 to run for Governor; now they were pounding him on the back; the impossible had happened! Gene LeBeuf's, "You've done it, Bobby Boy! " pierced through the excited babble. Sidney Aronovitz, the nephew of Mayor Abe Aronovitz, stood with a wistful expression on his face. Mr. Abe, who once said to Bob, "Someday you can be governor," had died six years before. It was apparent, as Bob and Sidney exchanged solemn smiles, of whom they were thinking.

Someone suggested it was time to go to the roof and accept the nomination, but Bob wanted to wait a little longer, for governor Burns had not yet conceded.

"I want to get hold of Jacksonville," he said, picking up the telephone. Three weeks ago he had made the same statement, swallowing an obvious concern; tonight there was only happiness in his voice, just a man wanting to call his friends and share his joy with them.

The High people in Jacksonville were tasting glory at long last. They had figured Bob needed at least 40% of their county's vote, and right now he was getting forty-three.

As the count swelled, so did the crowd. The faithfuls were there, bolstered by "Kelly for High" workers, and even a few of Governor Burns' supporters. Of the latter, one man said, "We had a county that came in 80% for Burns. Then a condominium in Miami votes and wipes out our whole county! "

Herman Terry was busy with figures. He smiled. In the city of Jacksonville Bob was getting over fifty percent of the vote. He smiled again.

The Magic City Explodes

Don Bruce was thinking about figures too, the ones with dollar signs in front of them. They had proved, beyond any doubt, that a man didn't need a couple of million dollars to be elected governor of Florida. Small ads in the Jacksonville papers asking for contributions of from one to one hundred dollars brought in floods of dollar bills; the highest single contribution from these was five dollars.

Don spoke for all of them. "As far as I'm concerned, the office of governor has been returned to the people."

A few shuddered, remembering the hate literature, the billboards, the terrible motorcade, the "Robert King High and convicted felon" ad. They had fought the undertow and survived. They earned their right to smile, for the voters were demonstrating they didn't care for gloves-off politics.

Earlier in the evening it became apparent to them that Burns was losing ground he could never recapture. In the 1964 race the Governor had won Baker, Bay, Bradford, Brevard, Collier, DeSoto, Hillsborough, Indian River, Leon, Martin, Nassau, Okeechobee, Orange, and Palm Beach counties. Tonight these were going to High.

By eight o'clock his Jacksonville supporters sensed a new governor. At that time the vote was 113,000 to 88,000; thirty-five minutes later the trend was sent, with Bob leading 271,994 to 199,869; ten more minutes passed, and their joy was almost unbearable: a reporter estimated that every Kelly vote in Palm Beach County had gone to Bob.

At ten o'clock they wept. The TV screen showed a picture that made the victory completely, undeniably real. Governor Burns was conceding.

"That's it," Bob said. "Get the Kellys. It's time to go."

There was a flurry as people gathered up jackets, purses, papers. The moment's activity smothered all feeling, and for an instant we became a roomful of gangling, writhing arms and legs, creatures without nerve, locked up tight against the panoply of emotion inside. How strange that the human mind would struggle against the reality of a dream long sought. But that was how it was. For a fraction of a second there was stillness and a kind of shudder. Victory brought a fateful awareness with it, a veiled glimpse of destiny. Whatever that destiny was, it was time to step out into it.

Suddenly the Kellys walked in. Scott's face was split horizontally with a big grin.

"I'm Haydon Burns, and I'll four-lane it! " He threw back his head and laughed, then gripped Bob's arm, a look of solemnity washing away his laughter. "It's great, Bob. Just great."

"Scott, I can't tell you how much I appreciate—" Bob's voice was husky; he included everyone in a sweeping glance. "All of you. Well—." The moment came. "Let's go! "

Bob took my hand and turned to look over his shoulder; I followed his gaze. The window, the blackness, the lights, the Magic City. Our eyes met, and we walked out the door. The curtain was about to go up on Act Three.

The corridor was lined with people on both sides, and plunked directly opposite us, looking like a three legged monster, was a huge television camera. Thick cables ran the length of the hallway and disappeared around the corner; I wondered insanely if they led all the way to the TV studio. Reporters had been waiting outside the suite since our arrival, and now they thrust microphones toward Bob, shouting to be heard.

"Could we have a few words, Mr. Mayor? "

"We can call you Governor now! "

"How does it feel? "

"I'm very happy," Bob beamed. "I'll have a statement just as soon as we can get upstairs."

Police officers began the difficult task of leading us through the corridor, to the stairway exit. Elevators were out of the question, they said; there were too many people waiting in front of them, anticipating their candidate's arrival, and we would never get through the crowd in one piece. So we walked up the two flights to the roof, sounding like a herd of elephants in an echo chamber.

We entered through the kitchen, but supporters had guessed this route, too; they were lined up against white walls and steel counters, perspiring from the heat of ovens, too many people, and too much excitement. Someone thrust a bouquet of roses in my arms; another brushed my cheek with a kiss as we were shoved forward. No longer were we walking; instead we were being inched through the kitchen.

The ballroom was a never-never land. A thousand people were stuffed into a room meant to hold several hundred, and as word spread that we were coming through the kitchen door, those people surged in one body. The policemen formed a wedge up ahead of us, pushing, straining, urging toward the stage; Bob had a fireman's grip on my wrist. I could not imagine that we were going anywhere, there was no floor space to walk on. The stage was set up not six feet from the kitchen exit, the length of a tall man, but it might as well have been a mile.

Finally, Bob was up, and from behind, an officer lifted me bodily and set me down next to my husband. It was like someone saying, "Would you please pass the salt?"

The spotlights, the camera lights, aimed at center stage. Bob was grinning with the wide open delight of a boy, the robust vitality of a man. He lifted his hand to the crowd and pandemonium broke loose.

A thousand throats tore open the room with a sound that was almost primeval, triggering a release of emotion. Their feelings, building up for months, had been laced up tight to make the suspense of election day bearable; now as their hometown candidate stood before them in victory, the cords of inhibition snapped.

A thousand bodies pressed toward the stage, arms reaching out for Bob, to touch, to grab, to pound on the back. In no other form of life is the sense of touch so important as in man; it tells of love, hate, joy, sorrow, and man feels cheated if he cannot express his passion by touching. So it was with the crowd. Let the candidate know how happy you are, communicate your inexpressible joy. Touch.

"Mr. Mayor! Mr. Mayor!"

A TV newscaster was trying desperately to get to Bob. He finally did, and though he stood right next to me, I couldn't hear a word he said. I was fascinated, however, by his appearance: the familiar clean-cut face was flushed and dripping, as if he'd stepped out of a pool; a lock of hair had fallen over his forehead, and his coat had given way to a once-starched shirt, now limp.

Bob's appearance, though we had been in the room only a few minutes, was not much better than the newscaster's; Scott Kelly looked like a tall tree being washed by rain. The heat and the noise and the crush were suffocating, and I began to feel giddy. Concentrate on one thing, I thought; stop looking at the dizzying sea of faces. And then the thing caught my eye. It had been there all along, sitting elegantly atop the wooden podium in front of us. A shiny, black name plate with white lettering. ROBERT KING HIGH, GOVERNOR. It made, as Bob once said, the unbelievable believable.

A hand from the crowd slipped a note across the podium. It contained the run-off figures: High, 596,471; Burns, 509,271. As a reporter said earlier, "The issue was no longer integrity. The issue was how much it would win by."

"Thank you, thank you." Bob was trying to quiet the people, ready to accept the nomination. "Okay! Thank you!" Slowly, like diminishing gale winds, the room became hushed, heavy with heat and contained breathing.

"I want to tell you," Bob said, "how grateful I am for the help of loyal supporters, for friends in every section of the state. The people who worked for this cause for two years when their only hope—the only reward they expected—was to do what they could to bring about a new beginning in the politics of this state.

"I don't know where my father is." Bob grinned. "I understand he's still in the Panhandle! Daddy? Wherever you are, please come home!" From somewhere in the crush Daddy High waved his arm, and the people cheered.

"I am grateful for all the support given by the great senator, Scott Kelly." Seven counties in the heart of Kelly Kountry switched to Bob in the run-off.

After the '64 election Bob remarked, "A man can afford to risk anything and everything for faith, for if he does not preserve that faith, he has lost everything." Now, two years later, his next words consummated that statement.

He leaned forward on the podium. Quietly, feelingly, he said, "Here tonight, I can swear before the Almighty One that I have not yielded to temptation. I have kept the faith.

"Let this election be a new beginning." His right hand started to chop the air. "Let us begin to honor integrity in all our public enterprises and politics. The work will not be done in a few years, nor even in my administration. Let us begin!"

Father and son conferring in the 1966 campaign

The room burned with cheers, the stage began to rock under the onslaught. Victory responded with near-hysteria as potted palms were knocked over and people were mashed against walls. Policemen quickly formed a cordon, digging in, straining every muscle to keep their arms locked against the rush. They were no longer protecting the Mayor of Miami. They were protecting the Democratic nominee for Governor of Florida.

They play still had six months to run, until the November general election, but for now, the curtain fell on Act Three.

Only two persons were missing on this night when the Magic City exploded. One was a salt-and-pepper haired gentleman who gave water to a seed that was yearning to grow. Mr. Abe. The other was a young man from Massachusetts who encouraged that seed to take root in deeper soil. John Kennedy. Their absence was felt. But so was their presence.

At last the Magic City, that young enchantress, yawned a sleepy smile, content with her love token to one of her own. One by one, her jewels came off. It was time to sleep.

CHAPTER THIRTEEN

Summer Song

Summertime, when the wind walks lazily across Biscayne Bay. Water skiers and fishing boats cut through the whitecaps, and oil-slicked bodies sprawl under the sun, making the beaches look like a giant parking lot for pink-baked jellyfish.

The school year comes to a screaming close as the final bell discharges thousands of yelling, whooping children, sneakers and freckles and pigtails flying down the street to join other sneakers and freckles and pigtails flying down the street.

Downtown Miami assumes a lethargy. Businessmen match their pace to the tempo of the tropics; secretaries have a longer coffee break, and if they are a few minutes late in the morning, no one really cares. It is too hot to care.

Summertime in the tropics is an opiate, a time when activity falls into a coma. Summertime is no time for politics.

But this year, summer sang a different song.

The *Miami Herald* put it bluntly: "IS GOVERNOR'S MANSION BIG ENOUGH FOR 8 HIGHS? Florida Democrats have a job, and now the question arises, is the Governor's Mansion big enough for Mr. High?"

Bob chuckled, still in the afterglow of victory; but for some unfathomable reason, the article made me want to pull myself into a cocoon, as if we were surrounded by peeping Toms.

The *Herald*'s speculation seemed premature but not illogical. In Florida, winning the Democratic nomination was tantamount to becoming governor; in almost a hundred years the Republicans had offered only token opposition, except in national elections. When supporters called Bob "Mr. Governor," even though the general election was months away, they were acting on a foregone conclusion.

Republicans didn't sound ready to lie down and die, however. They were saying this was their year, and their nominee, Claude Kirk of Jacksonville, echoed those sentiments. There was a growing disenchantment with the Democratic administration in Washington, and voters have been known to take their animosities out on whoever happens to be running. There were also rumors of a developing rift among state Democrats because of bitterness in the High-Burns race, and a split in the ruling party could help no one but the Republicans. This year, the elephant was ready to charge.

Victory carries its own brand of charisma. Everybody loves a winner, and we suddenly found ourselves with a multitude of friends and supporters eager to become part of the High team. Bob shrugged his shoulders, male fashion, at the Johnny-come-latelies. The Democratic nominee had too many important things to worry about than opportunists who suddenly wanted on the bandwagon. I could not ignore what was happening and floated from disgust to understanding for anything that breathed. Most of those who wanted to be near the winner were harmless, like the tired businessman who wanted a little of what he imagined was stardust to rub off on him.

There were about 28,000 original High workers throughout the state, and with the addition of Scott Kelly's people, newcomers boosted the figure to 50,000. But the door was not open to everyone who knocked.

One day, two elected officials brought a powerful lobbyist to Bob's office, offering support and favors. It was more than coincidence that the lobbyist represented an industry directed by the two officials. Their open wheeling and dealing was exceeded only by a liquor baron who came bearing a blank check; he wanted veto rights over future appointees. The manipulators, regardless of their diverse interests, had a startling parallelism; they saw no ethical wrong in their standards, or if they did, "good business" outweighed other considerations.

Among public officials who now offered their help, one face

was conspicuous by its absence: defeated Governor Haydon Burns. Many of his backers were openly contemptuous of Bob, and the Governor's support was the only thing that would make it easier for the Burns people to vote for High in November. But a Burns endorsement of Claude Kirk, the Republican candidate, would split wide open the already-mumbling Democratic party. Though defeated, the Governor held the whip hand. And he was silent.

Not a few High supporters resented Burns, saying, "What do we want his support for? We don't even need it." But as Don Petit kept repeating, in politics one must be practical.

In the middle of June, Petit went to Tallahassee. He met with a Burns intimate, probing the ticklish problem of getting the Governor to support Bob; the Governor was said to be coldly furious, and his support would have to be won gradually, if at all. Burns' friend believed he could persuade the Governor to invite Bob to the upcoming National Governor's Conference, a courtesy gesture toward his party's nominee. It was worth a try, Don agreed, so he left Tallahassee, relieved that his efforts might open an avenue between the Governor and Bob.

The ax fell when Petit arrived in Miami. He learned that that very same day Scott Kelly had been to see the Governor. Burns still smarted over Kelly's "Big Lie" tag, not to mention his support of Bob, and most of the hour they spent together was in heated discussion. Burns did agree to see Bob.

With a sinking feeling his own solution was going out the window, Don conceded there was no choice but to follow through with the appointment and hope Bob's interview progressed better than Kelly's. But why, oh why, he wondered, didn't someone let him know of Kelly's visit in advance? It was an increasingly disturbing element in the campaign, a case of the right hand not knowing what the left was doing.

Bob went to see Burns, and after a two hour conference emerged from the Governor's office.

A reporter dashed up. "Is the Governor going to endorse you, Mayor High?"

Bob shrugged.

"Why did you come here, personally, to seek his support?"

"Out of respect for the opinions of the nearly half a million people who voted for Governor Burns," Bob replied. "I think it would require that."

At home, tired and defeated-looking, Bob said it was the worst two hours he had ever spent. The Governor was nearly irrational in his tirade over Kelly, he said, and he still believed Senator Robert Kennedy had financed Bob's campaign.

A few hours later speculation ended. There would be no endorsement of Robert King High coming from Tallahassee. The whip hand had cracked.

Peace River Ranch. The name seemed manufactured for the purpose of the conclave. An idyllic home in citrus country near Frostproof, Florida, the private retreat for Scott Kelly's finance chairman, now co-finance chairman of the High campaign. Cars streamed toward Frostproof from all over the state bearing High and Kelly chairmen. Their destination: Peace River Ranch and a summit meeting, where both factions could be successfully merged into a winning team in November. And a peaceful one, for already the claws were being sharpened.

After the second primary win, some of the High people decided it was time to "write Kelly and his group off." Others, and Bob was one of those, saw no reason for not bringing in everyone. After all, they said, we want to win. Neither could Bob erase Scott's help; to have written him off would have been unthinkable, and at any suggestion of this, he replied, "Are you out of your mind? "

Insiders came to call the meeting The Marriage Feast. It was essential that the two factions be unified, so Bob and Don Petit met with county chairmen two at a time, a High man and a Kelly man, asking them to assume a co-chairmanship of their particular county. Several fumed, walked out, came back in, and the procedure would begin again.

A High man said, "Bob, we're for you 100 percent, but the Kelly people have no respect for us. They're trying to take over." This was the crux of the matter.

There were personal and philosophical differences between the two groups, and it began to look as if dual chairmanships would create more internal problems, instead of solving them.

Intrigue ran deep. If a High man wanted a Kelly man's attention, he didn't simply call him; he caught his eye and nodded furtively toward a corner. "It was like playing 'Let's Make a Deal! " someone said. Still another High man walked around mumbling to himself, "Don't know why we have to take 'em in. We beat 'em! "

Bud Stack, Bob's law partner, was approached by a couple of Kelly men. They thought their people should have fifty percent of everything, they said.

Bud thought a minute. "You want fifty percent of nothing? Sure! "

Finally, the two factions agreed to work together. They differed, however, on the campaign's timing. The Kelly people wanted to continue full steam; most of the High group, led by Petit, wanted to slack off campaigning for the summer.

We don't want to do anything major now, Don contended, even the voters need a rest! No dialogue of consequence, at least until Labor Day. That would be a good time to crank up. So Don left Peace River Ranch for New York, intending to return in late summer when he'd get them ready to win in November! It was the right plan, Don thought, and he was still campaign manager, wasn't he?

But it was the beginning of a change, a slow pulling apart of factions, for the currents that swell within men were already at work; they began with a taste of victory. Peace River Ranch was an unlikely name.

The flat lands swelled into rolling countryside, and soon the highway, undulating beneath the rays of the sun, rose and vanished ahead of us in an inverted V. Bob and I were in the hill country, the mountains. He remarked wistfully that we were in the land of Thomas Wolfe, and I smiled. He never tired of quoting from *You can't Go Home Again,* especially, ". . . The promise of America." It was like telling his own story in a few words.

Our destination was Williamsburg, Virginia, and we sped through North Carolina without stopping. Even so, it was an elixir. The emerald green of the farmlands, the blue-gray of the mountains, the purity of the air—all began working their old magic. Most glorious of all, politics was a million miles away.

Summer Song

Apart from seeking the governorship, Bob was a student of politics; he drove himself to exhaustion, but the fascination, the lure, the art of the profession glistened underneath like an uncut gem. My saturation point was not nearly so high. By the time the Peace River Ranch conclave rolled away, my mind was like a sponge dripping with an overdose of politics, and it needed wringing out. So we were stealing a week away from endorsements and speeches, far from the shores of Florida.

The countryside had its effect on Bob, too. The tired lines around his eyes were beginning to relax; the preoccupied glint now meant he was solely concerned with passing every car on the road (the car was a giant concession to me; Bob hated going anywhere unless he could fly). He joked a lot, watching me carefully for a response. He was trying so hard to convince me his mind wasn't on the governor's race!

We were getting far away from home, not only for a change, but for anonymity, for a quiet dinner without a "Hello there, Mayor!" I should have known better!

We stopped at a motel, Bob secured our room, then drove the car around to it and started unloading luggage. Suddenly the door next to ours opened, and a man wearing bermuda shorts emerged.

"Why-y-y! Aren't you the Mayor of Miami?"

"Yes," Bob grinned, extending his hand. He was enjoying being recognized. "Are you from Florida?"

"Sure am! How about that? Have to come to Virginia to meet the next Governor of Florida—and the First Lady!"

I pried my lips into something resembling a smile.

The same thing happened in Williamsburg. Bob and I entered the Inn for dinner, when a family at a nearby table jumped to their feet. "Look who's here! The Mayor of Miami!" Other heads began to turn, curiously. Ah, how nice it was to get away from it all!

It reminded me of a trip during the '64 campaign, when my friends and I were winding up a Bandwagon tour. We were driving home and decided to have a leisurely dinner at some quiet restaurant, away from reporters and crowds. We removed our High buttons and entered a lovely, candlelit restaurant.

The hostess smiled. "Well! Don't you girls look cute! Are you singers or something?"

Mayor High relaxing in the country

I felt the blood rush to my face at our stupidity. We had taken such pains to remove the High buttons—our traces of identity—but we ignored the fact we were all dressed alike!

"No, no, we're not singers. We are campaigning." I was almost whispering.

"Oh, how nice! Who are you campaigning for?"

And of course, we had to tell her.

During dinner a young man with microphone and tape recorder approached our table. "I beg your pardon, aren't you Mrs. Robert King High?" I nodded, and he continued. "Well, how nice you ladies stopped here! We do a local radio program from the restaurant. I wonder if I might take a minute of your time?"

The poor man looked bewildered at our hysterical laughter.

There had been no escape then, and it looked as if we could not lose ourselves in Virginia either. But we tried, and I learned something new about Bob in the process: he could almost forget the present in his preoccupation with history. The Governor's Palace in Williamsburg held a special fascination.

"Let's see now," Bob said, looking at our tour book. "What is this place?"

"The Governor's Palace." Then I caught the twinkle in his eye!

The crowning point came on the trip back home; it was at Monticello, the architectural triumph of Thomas Jefferson. Bob's boyhood idol never shone more strongly than on that sunny afternoon. His carefully measured steps seemed to say, I am walking where he walked; occasionally, during an explanation of a particular point by our guide, Bob nodded, as if to himself—*Yes, that is how it would have happened;* he gazed, with something akin to awe, at Jefferson's forward-looking inventions.

During a stroll in the gardens, he turned to me. "Faith, can you imagine, can you just imagine—? " The question groped and remained unfinished.

During an exchange on the veranda one of the tourists, a heavy-set man with jaws clamped on an unlit cigar, exclaimed, "Say! Did everybody know Thomas Jefferson didn't have a damn thing to do with the Declaration of Independence? S'one of the biggest hoaxes in the history of America! "

A dead quiet dropped on the group, and Bob stiffened; he had gone white around the mouth, a High sign of controlled rage. Our guide told the tourist that if he had proof of his statement, he should notify the proper authorities, she was sure they would be most interested. But from Bob, I caught a muttered, "Damn ugly American."

As we walked down the gravel drive, we turned to look back. The moment was revealing, for it seemed that a bit of the greatness of the Jeffersonian era of democracy was deep inside Bob High, and there was no doubt he left a part of himself at Monticello.

The promise of America.

Problems, problems. Don Petit was still in New York, and during his absence the campaign didn't lack for commanders. That was the trouble, the old, old cliché of too many chiefs and not enough Indians; but it was enough to act as the catalyst for a multitude of crises waiting to erupt.

In early summer word went out that former Burns supporters were not welcome in the High campaign. After Bob denied the report, workers from the Governor's camp began coming over. But the damage was already done, with the result that many Burns people were made to feel like unwanted stepchildren. Sensitive feelings on both sides were understandable; why should the Burns followers want to work side by side with people who didn't like them before they knew them? And why indeed would High people, after so many episodes, welcome with open arms those they felt were responsible for that bitterness?

Burns workers were finally absorbed into county groups, but the main organizational problem remained the divided camps of High and Kelly: the Marriage Feast had merely bought a little time. With supporters from the three different groups, plus aides from the offices of several state cabinet members, there was ample personnel and a wealth of experience to make a topnotch organization—if they would all pull in the same direction. But more and more High people repeated, "Bob, we just can't work with the Kelly men. I tell you, they're trying to take over! " And the Kelly supporters responded, "That's ridiculous! They read all sorts of intrigue into everything we say! " Typically, there was truth on both sides.

Bob reacted with mixed emotions. The pressures of campaigning were undiminished, yet he found himself thrust in the additional role of peacemaker. It was like being caught in a crossfire, listening to the complaint of first one, then another. His frustration was apparent as he tried to smooth two sets of feathers, while keeping friendships intact. Bob didn't want to hurt anyone's feelings—to an extreme, it was said—and a firmer hand could have erased the petty quarrels. But Bob wanted people to like him, a simple motive which produced complicated results.

Simplicity flies out the window in politics; emotions, complex personalities, and even more complex situations, abound. I had finally come to understand that Democrats and Republicans have widely differing philosophies (I could never see why; they both ate, slept, and breathed, didn't they?); I was now trying to comprehend the divergent beliefs within the state Democratic Party itself. Basically, they were liberal and conservative, with all shades of gray in between, and it was these divergencies which led to the campaign's next unanswered question. What should be the candidates's image?

Those who concerned themselves with images and image-making decided the Miami mayor might not appeal to the "conservative" north Floridian as he did to the big-city voter. It was necessary to play down Bob's metropolitan image, they said, and there was no

Summer Song

time to lose. This was primarily the philosophy of the Kelly forces.

There was another side. The original High people, including the campaign manager, felt the image-makers were wrong. To try and change Bob's image would be too dramatic a move; it would create the need for a complete voter reeducation program, and there was not enough time for that. For the moment they were satisfied with keeping the vote percentages Bob already had, and at all costs they didn't want to destroy the 82.3% who lived in urban Florida.

"Don't chase rainbows," they cautioned. Besides, there was the most important element of all. Bob High was what he was.

While image debates continued, other meetings began. Pie-cutting sessions. The birds of a feather were flocking to their own, as new alliances and uneasy friendships formed; in lowered voices, men discussed the positions they wanted when Bob went to Tallahassee. We learned there were several spreading the word they were going to be State Beverage Director—an interesting predicament. One made his pronouncement in a crowded downtown elevator; another could have been counted on to consume so much himself, there would be no beverage left to direct!

Nevertheless, the pie-cutters talked. It was an interesting phenomenon, a disease peculiar to politics. A campaign is no place for those who have not built up an immunity to the disease, for it is contagious. Sometimes even the most untarnished of campaigners lose their artlessness once they become seasoned; their innocence, not unlike the arteries, begins to harden. An eager young man, fresh out of college, asks to work in a campaign and does so with enthusiasm and sincerity; two years later the clean-cut look is still there, but his eyes glint while they measure a co-worker as a help or hindrance to his own ambition; he's busy now, much too busy to be bothered with trivia, and his friendly smile gives way to a self-important smirk. "Got to rush this out for the candidate. He depends on me, you know."

The disease is not limited to men. In a sense the woman is worse, for her once-gracious candor becomes as false as the techniques of a public relations expert trying to sell a hairbrush to a bald man.

Then there are the few men and women strangely drawn to

politics because of boredom or unhappy marriages. Good workers many, but in reality their performance is another way of trying to prove their masculinity or feminity to themselves and others. One or two may have joined a campaign looking for a healthy escape from a lifeless marriage, but if that is the underlying motive, all too often they become reckless and their diversions an emotional trap. They form the habit of floating from campaign to campaign, still searching for themselves.

The crisis of the moment centered around Scott Kelly. The day after Bob won the Democratic nomination, a reporter asked Kelly if he was going to step out of the campaign.

"No," Scott replied. "I'll be campaigning for Bob High. I'm going to be as active as he wants me to be."

Privately, Kelly let it be known he wanted to travel with Bob, rather than take the campaign trail alone. And for a while, he did. Bob enjoyed Scott; he considered him a friend. But others, campaign personnel and reporters, voiced suspicions that Kelly's motives were more pro-Kelly than High; certainly, they argued, candidate High would draw the bulk of cameras and publicity, and anyone who happened to be with him would share the spotlight.

"If we can just convince Kelly he hasn't been elected Governor," they said.

Practical politics dictated the value of Kelly's presence in the campaign. Bob was again running against a conservative, a man who would doubtless cut into his votes in known Republican counties; it followed that Scott and his "Kelly Kountry" would be helpful. On the other hand, Kelly was not overwhelmingly popular in south Florida, a High stronghold, and too much Kelly here could turn into a liability. Aides suggested the effectiveness of the tough ex-football player would have to be weighed carefully, so after several weeks, his travels with Bob began to taper off.

Speculation over Kelly was a bitter pill for Bob during these months. In 1964 Bob said, "A friend is tolerant of a friend." Now he answered his critics with a touch of reproof. "Scott Kelly is more than a political ally. He is a friend."

Speechwriter Don Wilkes was next in line to become a bone of contention. On the night of July 22, he accompanied Bob and me to a Kick-Off banquet, hosted by the state Democratic Party. The sky was a huge, black water faucet, and we sat in our car, in a line of a hundred or more, waiting to drive under the entrance of Miami Beach's Deauville Hotel. Bob drummed impatient fingers on the side of the car and peered through the "swish" of windshield wipers at harried parking attendants who slammed car doors and screeched away to the hidden parking arena.

"Whaht a pity! " said Don. "The guest of honah is missing his own reception." He asked if Bob wanted to go over his speech again while we waited.

Bob accepted the sheaf of papers, but he was irritated; he had seen the speech for the first time only thirty minutes before, and tonight's address before the still-quarreling Democratic Party members was an important one. He liked to have ample time to go over his speeches and make any necessary changes, and Wilkes' last-minute timing was becoming increasingly frustrating. He said little , however, because he liked Don and recognized his talent.

Others complained bitterly. Wilkes had begun traveling with Bob, and supporters were suspicious.

"He's like a watchdog," they said. "Jealous of anyone who tries to talk with Bob. He's just afraid of losing his influence! " Besides, they added, he talks like Shakespeare. And that explained everything.

Unfortunately it did not explain the scramble for position, the jockeying of cliques within cliques, as members eyed one another with anxiety. Unholy alliances. And Wilkes, they accused, was an alliance of one.

The line of cars began to move, and we finally reached the hotel entrance and the banquet. In terms of people and the campaign kitty, the dinner was a packed success: over 1,000 attended, swelling the financial profit to $50,000.

With the glaring exception of Governor Burns, every ranking Democrat in the state turned out, bringing their entourages and handshakes and smiles with them. They also brought their divergent philosophies, bits and pieces gathered from all over Florida— but one would never have known it. All was happiness and harmony; they were going to pull together for the good of the party and the candidate, they said.

It sounded more and more like Peace River Ranch.

Republican nominee Claude Kirk lived in Jacksonville, the home of Governor Burns. The two shared another interest: many of Burns' Democratic supporters, quietly or otherwise, went to Kirk's side.

The High camp generally agreed that the campaign in the remaining months should not be run as it was in the primaries because there was no public record on Kirk, and at a meeting in late summer, opposite viewpoints on strategy were discussed.

Claude Kirk had no political record, and Bob had scratched six pages of a recent speech because they bordered on a personal attack. Bill Baggs expressed concern; like Bob, he knew personal attacks were ill-advised.

"I think the best way to handle Claude Kirk," he drawled, "is to ignore him."

Bill's opinion was shared by others, the campaign manager and national Democrats among them. Florida Senator Spessard Holland had been challenged by Kirk in 1964, and in his speeches the Senator never even mentioned his name. He, too, advised, "Ignore him!"

Not so with Scott Kelly. "Go after Kirk!" The camp, as usual, was divided.

Bob found his familiar underdog position reversed. As the Democratic nominee, he was suddenly the heavyweight; but against a man who had no public record, it was more like shadow-boxing. As far as he was concerned, at least the issues remained unchanged. Education. The imbalance of real property taxes. Elimination of waste and inefficiency in government. A competitive bid system.

Again, he would ask for a code of ethics and conflict of interest law. "To prevent the public men," he said, "from exploiting public business for private gain."

He wanted a ceiling on campaign expenditures to keep money from deciding elections, and a strict lobbying act to deter lobbyists who might attempt to corrupt the legislative processes. As it was in the beginning, integrity was still the issue.

Kirk said he would ask for no new taxes, and that he would make Florida first in education. He would "have a position on everything before the campaign was over" in a series of "white papers." Then he said something that was appallingly reminiscent.

"Florida will sink in the shadow of 'me-tooism' if the ultra-liberal side wins."

It was the tip-off to the coming three months. Ultra-liberal. In an effort to dispel this image all over again, Bob scheduled meetings with citizen groups in north Florida and actively sought the support of public officials who wore the conservative tag.

An adviser was worried, particularly that Kelly was influencing Bob toward a more rural image."Look," he said, "Kelly believes a man has to be a conservative to win a state-wide position, but that's not so! " Bob beat Kelly and Burns, both conservatives, he added. Nevertheless, Bob's trips into north Florida continued, and he was back to twenty-hour days.

I was among those who rebelled at summer campaigning and grumbled about a particular dinner Bob and I had to attend. But the evening developed one of the wierdest twists I'd ever experienced. I was in the powder room, trying to exit through a crowd of forty or fifty women, when a voice said, "I beg your pardon. Aren't you Mrs. Bob High? "

I started to turn around when a voice from behind me said, "Yes, I am."

I listened spellbound.

"I just want you to know how much I admire your husband, Mrs. High! "

"Thank you," 'Mrs. High' said.

"Does he ever get a chance to sleep? "

"Oh yes! We have all those children, you know! "

I cringed. Ah, politics!

The dinners and the trips endured, and all at once the campaign took a slight upturn. Unity began to spread in the Democratic Party like slow molasses, and the lines to Miami were hot with messages of new support. Bob was endorsed by the political arm of the Florida Education Association, and eventually by the leaders of the Florida House and Senate, all but one member of the Congressional delegation, four former governors, the Republican gubernatorial candidate of 1960, Senators Spessard Holland and George Smathers, seventeen newspapers, and the sheriffs of fifteen Panhandle counties. These endorsements generated more support, and by the end of July a poll released new figures: High, 51%; Kirk, 34%; Undecided, 15%. The steeplechase was on.

Bob alighted from the plane clutching the hand of our daughter, Holly. The sparkle in her eyes outshone the copper in her hair. "I got his autograph! " she whispered.

"Whose? " I teased.

"The President's! " She looked at me with all the reproach a ten-year-old could muster.

Bob had attended a conference at the White House, and this trip was Holly's turn. He made it a point to take each of our children, as they became old enough, on trips with him and had made the circuit through Bobby and our three oldest girls several times.

Holly and I went home to discuss the White House, and Bob headed for a press conference. He was about to make a startling announcement.

"This is a good day for me, personally," he said. "This is a good day for my candidacy for the governorship. This is a good day for Florida.

"I want to announce the appointment of Scott Kelly as my state campaign chairman for the general election."

Reporters asked how the appointment came about. "The answer is simple. I drafted Scott Kelly. He has proven he is a man of his word."

Bob said that in terms of practical politics, Kelly's appointment meant the campaign would be organized with precision. Party unity was also a factor.

"I drafted Scott Kelly," he concluded, "because he is my friend."

The appointment would have no effect on Petit's role as campaign manager. Petit was still working in New York, but when he returned, he would continue as campaign manager. The distinction between the two was that Kelly would provide general direction, while Petit would command the day-to-day operation.

Kelly moved to Miami for the duration of the campaign. Those under him worked out of the thirteenth floor of the Ferré Building; those under Petit had the fifteenth. But more than a floor separated the two groups.

In the waning days of summer, Flat Creek, Tennessee, became the setting for one of the most unusual political rallies ever held by a candidate for Governor of Florida. Surrounded by the gently rolling hills of the Cumberland Valley, decked with farms, a white-steepled country church, and a square, it was reminiscent of springtime politicking in the Florida Panhandle. There was a wispish fancy about the spot, the fleeting sensation you get that you have been in a place before, smelled a particular fragrance but don't remember when.

A large "Welcome Home, Bob High" banner stretched across State Highway 82. The cavalcade of a hundred cars, wearing Tennessee and Florida license plates, "High for Governor" bumper stickers, and "High Family Day" signs, motored through the Shelbyville square and looped over hills to Flat Creek and the school grounds.

Riding in an open convertible and grinning to match the late-August sun was Bob, returned to his native hills. As the caravan pulled onto the school grounds, he exclaimed, "Look at that! "

Nearly 2,000 people were milling around—in the hill country there was room for that many to mill—and a giant tent, like those used for evangelical meetings, sheltered tables and chairs, men, women, and children. A large bunting-wrapped platform with microphones and loudspeakers was being used at that moment by a troupe of performers from the Grand Ole Opry. Flat Creek had turned out en masse to honor its native son, and the air reverberated with the rich twang of the hills.

"Bob High Day" had been in the planning stages since the closing weeks of 1965, and Flat Creek was as delighted as Bob. Back at the beginning, at the law office meeting when the "Integrity" theme was set, Flat Creek Day was discussed. It was a nebulous idea then, not much more than a thought, and it was triggered by the sample brochure bearing the words, "That Feller From Flat Creek." For the time being the idea was shelved, but when Bob won the Democratic nomination, the plans were picked up again.

Some argued the idea was not sound, saying Bob should identify as a Floridian, not a Tennessean. Others believed it would be of great value in influencing the rural vote, Bob's weakest area. Bob himself looked on the idea with the glee of a boy on Christmas Eve.

Bob and five of our children flew to Tennessee, and I drove up with a friend. After 800 miles I was almost ready to board a plane, but not quite. Later, I learned there were fifty-seven others who shared my sentiments.

A large group had boarded a DC-7 at Miami International early in the morning for the flight to Tennessee. Anyone would have known the DC-7 belonged to the High group; it looked like an injured old buzzard, all scotch-taped together. The plane made it to Orlando, a necessary stop to pick up more supporters and members of the press.

Herman Terry and Don Bruce were among those who boarded at Orlando. At the door of the plane, Herman noticed smoke coming out from under one of the wheels. Oh well, maybe it was supposed to do that. Inside it was hot, so hot that most of the men removed their coats.

As they took off Don was looking out the window. "Hey! " he called out. "This bird sure does rattle! Anything wrong? "

"Nah! " came the reply.

"Then why is oil splashing up all over my window? "'

Sure enough, the oil was there. But they all laughed; they were in a party mood.

At 600 feet the plane began to shudder.

"One of the engines is out! Look! It's smoking! "

In a moment the pilot's voice came over the intercom. "We are experiencing a little difficulty and are going to turn back."

The old plane banked into a turn. No one was laughing now, and fifty-seven faces pressed to the windows, watching the airport beneath them, fire trucks racing toward the runway. Hands unconsciously tightened seat belts.

First reports had the plane crash landing, but the old gooney bird was lucky and so were its passengers. On the ground in Orlando, there was a rush on telephones—reporters to phone in stories, others to tell relatives they were safe. While aides scurried to round up other aircraft, the group unwound in the airport coffee shop.

"Wasn't it nice of old Claude (Kirk) to loan Bob that airplane? "

"Where's the LSD machine? " somebody asked. "We can make it under our own power that way! "

Aides succeeded in locating two twin-engine Pipers and asked the reporters if they wanted to draw lots for the available seats.

Summer Song

As one columnist later reported, "It weren't that we was nervous or anything like that because of a little old emergency landing with two fire engines standing by. We just didn't want to break the law by participating in one of them illegal drawings! " But like the mail, nothing deterred the press.

Someone located an Orlando executive on the golf course, and he agreed to lend his Gulfstream prop jet to the rest of the party. They were already four hours late and had no breakfast or lunch, but they were in the air again. They landed on the one runway in Shelbyville and rode a school bus at sixty miles an hour over mountain curves to Flat Creek. With the arrival of the last of the Rumpled Retinue, the program got under way.

Half the people there were related in one way or another, and Daddy High led the list of those ready to pop their buttons with pride. He was going from group to group, telling his latest story.

"Did you hear about the man who was speakin' to a predominantly Republican crowd?

"He asked, 'Is there a Democrat in the audience? " and one man raised his hand. Then he said, 'Come up to the microphone and tell us why you're a Democrat.'

"We-e-ll, the man came up, and he said, 'I guess the reason I'm a Democrat is because my daddy, and grandaddy, and all before him were.'

"The speaker looked him in the eye and said, 'If they were horse thieves, I guess you'd be a horse thief, then.'

"The man thought a minute and replied, 'No-o-o . . . I guess then I'd be a Republican! "

Reporters kept saying Daddy High was one of a kind. They noticed how his eyes followed his son through the crowd, how he nodded to himself when he saw the pleasure on his son's face as he greeted old friends. Just over the hill was the barn Daddy High had built fifty years before, almost as good as new. In a way, he was like that barn; solid, endurable, a part of the land.

Everyone was filled with fried chicken, biscuits, and all the trimmings, ready to hear the speeches, and the crowd settled back, turning expectant faces to the platform. Four of the chairs on the platform were occupied by former governors of Tennessee, and one of the notables was Senator Albert Gore.

"When Bob High left the farm to go to the city," he said, "we were worried. When he became a lawyer and joined the Phillistines and the Pharisees, we really began to wrinkle our brow. But when he became Mayor of that metropolitan slot-machine, we almost gave up hope!

"But now he's redeemed himself by being nominated by the Democrats of that great state of Florida! "

Bob stepped to the microphone. "I thank you, the good and kindly people of Flat Creek and Bedford County, for such a homecoming.

"Some say that Flat Creek does not appear on most road maps, that it is not big enough. Whether it appears on road maps or not, Flat Creek now occupies a prominent place on the political map of Florida! " Cheers.

"I am not positive my nomination made so much history. But I will be elected Governor in November.

"My rise from farm boy to nominee for Governor is a true example of what our country is all about.

"Thomas Wolfe said you can't go home again." And he paused. "I have come home."

CHAPTER FOURTEEN

A Camp Divided

'Tis ten to one this play can never please all that are here. The last act was approaching, and those who waited in the wings grew restless. One false step, one miscue, and the whole play could come crashing down around their heads. After months of building the production, the players' strangled emotions found release in convulsive outbreaks. With the November election only a month and a half away, Don Petit walked out.

Bob and I were in Gainesville with the Kellys to attend the University of Florida Homecoming. After the game we returned to our motel, where a long distance message awaited Bob. He placed the call.

"What?" His expression grew suddenly grim. "My God, when?"

In a few moments, he replaced the receiver, sat slumped with his head between his hands. He looked up at me. "Petit's walked out!"

"Walked out? You mean—quit the campaign?"

He nodded. "Just like that. My God!" Then he got mad. "How the hell could he do that to me? He's supposed to be a professional!"

Here the election was, a little over a month away, he said. What was he going to do now? The least Don could have done was to call him personally. Surely the whole mess was not that bad. But no, he'd already talked to reporters, and now the campaign's internal problems would be aired for the public. How would the public feel, he wondered, about a candidate whose organization seemed to be falling apart? He answered his own question. "Not much of a leader, that's what they'll think! "

"What are you going to do? "

"Oh, I don't know, I . . . oh, Hell! " The word was wrapped in disgust and resignation. For one thing, he'd catch the first plane home. Maybe he could convince Petit to come back.

Within minutes he was on his way to the airport, but before he could reach Miami, the story broke in the papers.

Petit's statement began, "The manager believes that his approach to a campaign based primarily on mass communications and intense campaigning activity in the urban areas differs dramatically from the Kelly approach of campaigning almost entirely in the rural areas."

Since June, Petit said, he had been completely frustrated over internal problems. "The High people believe, as I believe, that a total unified front is necessary to win the November election.

"The supporters of Governor Burns who are eager to lend their support to Mayor High are being prevented from doing so by the forces of Senator Scott Kelly." And Bob relied heavily, he said, on Kelly's advice.

Of Bob, he stated, "I don't want to hurt him in any way. This will give him an opportunity to reorganize and get someone else, someone neutral to manage his campaign. I want to give him the benefit of my thinking, for whatever it may be worth."

A reporter asked if he might decide to return as campaign manager. "I don't feel effective any longer," he replied.

"Will you refuse to return, even if Mayor High requests it? "

"I'm afraid I have to in the interests of the campaign." As a parting shot, he added, "Some High supporters believe Scott Kelly has claimed just about everything but winning the first primary for High."

The crux of the matter boiled down to one word. Kelly.

Scott's only comment was, "We have a job to do, we are following a plan set out in June, and it is on schedule." And that's that, the tone said.

Bob, in his own press conference, acknowledged there were personality clashes among his original workers and the Kelly forces.

A Camp Divided

"There was an honest conflict of judgment as to how the campaign should be conducted. Petit had very earnest feelings that I should campaign one way, and I wanted to do it another way.

"It's true that there are not as many people in the rural areas. But I made the decision to campaign in the grass roots with town hall meetings, so that I could know first hand the problems of every section. It was a judgment I had to make. I have made it and will continue to make the decisions."

Since June, Bob had been into forty of Florida's sixty-seven counties. "This is time consuming," he said, "and the candidate is away for periods of time. This perhaps does cause a lack of communication.

"But I intend to be Governor of Florida, and that means every part of Florida." He added he had not received official notification of the resignation from Don, but they were going to meet and try to iron things out right away.

There were instant repercussions. In Pensacola, six members of the campaign walked out. "We are for Bob High one hundred percent," they said, "but we're backing Petit in this thing. Petit could heal our situation if he stays in the campaign. If he leaves, we're in trouble."

A long build-up of situations and personality clashes led to Petit's walkout. One incident occurred back in June, at a meeting of the Democratic Executive Committee in Clearwater. Word reached Bob and Petit in Miami that Kelly and some of his men were attempting to oust the present chairman of the Committee in favor of someone else, and that they were saying this was the wish of the new Democratic nominee, Bob High. Not so, Bob said, and he and Petit left for Clearwater.

When they arrived, there was a new chairman of the Democratic Executive Committee. Petit called it a power grab, but it was too late to do anything about it.

He was concerned. They didn't need the power structure, the politicos. The courthouse crowd gave only lip service to a candidate, and when the chips were down, they gave little of that. In the '64 race the power structure had nothing to gain, but now Bob was the Democratic nominee, and greed brought an attempt at undercutting anyone close to him.

There was a distinct need to reach the people who had voted against Burns, rather than for High, but internal frustrations left less and less time to deal with the larger problem of winning. One man, a constant needler, spread the story that Bob was going to fire Petit; Bob discovered that several workers had used campaign money for such items as a weekend excursion and a color TV; after a dispute, Kelly asked two men, on loan from the Secretary of State's office, to leave; schedules were changed or cancelled at the last minute, often without Bob or Don's knowledge. And then there was the question of rural versus urban campaigning. To Petit, the frustrations were like a rock in his shoe. And he wanted to get rid of the rock.

Bob met with Don, but he could not persuade him to change his mind. Don did say he would try to heal some of the wounds caused by the split between High and Kelly forces.

It was said that Petit's walkout was not worthy of a professional campaign manager, that it was scandalous. For a professional, that was so; for a human being, it was understandable.

To the papers Bob said, "I have accepted his resignation. He's worked hard for me, and I stand ready to help him in any way I can."

Privately, he was demoralized yet caught in the middle, between Petit and Kelly. And again, he wanted harmony with both. In a way, he was lucky. Had he felt and reacted differently, the campaign might have been shattered then and there. But it picked itself up and headed for November.

Bob didn't have time to worry about a replacement for Don and announced he would manage his own campaign. In only a matter of days, he saw it was impossible to be both candidate and manager, so he sat down at the telephone and called his Orange County Chairman, Bill Poorbaugh, one of his closest friends.

"Poorboy?"

"Hello, hello! How's it going?"

"How does it look to you?"

"I think things are shapin' up, Bobby. I've been figuring the odds again, and they look pretty good!"

Bill would live and die by the odds, and Bob chuckled. "Bill, I can't manage this thing. I don't have the time. Can you come

A Camp Divided 185

down here and act as State Coordinator until it's over? I need someone I can trust."

It took Poorboy about three-tenths of a second to form his answer. "Sure, I will! and Bob," there was a pause, "if it works out, fine! If not, and you want to ship me back to Orange County, don't worry about it. It won't hurt my feelings."

Bob hung up the receiver with a contented sigh. "Good ole Poorboy." If there was anyone who could maintain harmony, it was Poorboy, he mused. So many prima donnas.

Bob and Bill's friendship had spanned twenty years. It didn't matter that Poorboy was not a politician, not a pro; he became the new coordinator because he had sound judgment, and because Bob trusted him. Amazingly, no one walked out when he came to take over.

He was on long distance constantly, catering, soothing the instant uproars. And instant they were. Scoop up emotion, any emotion, add more than one person, and voilà! Instant uproar. Some of the college students in Gainesville talked of dropping out of the campaign; they were being "pushed around by the Kelly Kommandoes." Poorboy said, "I know how you feel, but think of Bob. You're in it for him."

In his own county, conservative Orange, a group with liberal leanings pronounced themselves county chairmen, they were taking over. Conservatives said, "Just try it! " Poorboy admonished gently.

In Fort Lauderdale, a Keystone Kops situation arose. Two High workers who had manned the headquarters there since the beginning were told a young Kelly man was coming in to devote full time to managing the office; their own positions would remain unchanged, they were told, but misunderstandings developed. Converted Burns people said, "Don't let the Kelly men in! " Another faction wanted to kick out the treasurer, a High man, because he sided with the Burns people; there were tears and recriminations. "Look! I sympathize with you," Poorboy said. "But listen to the odds I've figured on Bob's chances in your county," and he rattled off a string of promising figures. "A situation like you all have there could kill those figures, you know that! " They listened. In most cases, Poorboy said later, each person had honestly done what he thought was right. Anyway, he gave them the benefit of the doubt.

More than a few incidents, however, had the distrubing element of viciousness at their root. This was not especially true in the '64 race, when personality conflicts seemed almost comical. Such an incident quickly made the rounds in the High camp that year.

One of the men on the finance committee, a tall, wiry bundle of explosives, kept up a running dispute with another co-worker; the only thing they agreed on was the candidate's name. On this particular day, he burst into campaign headquarters, thrust his hand in his pocket and pulled out $500, a contribution he had just picked up—and flung the money on the floor!

"What are you doing, what's the matter with you?" somebody asked, scrambling to pick up the flying bills.

"Where is he? Where is he?" He was mad at his hated co-worker again and headed down the hall for Hated Co-worker's office yelling, "Come on out! I'll fight you! Come out and settle it like a man!"

Hated Co-Worker locked his office door and would not come out.

"You come out of there and I'll throw you out the window!" Hated Co-Worker went on with his business, secure behind his door.

Then, for reasons best known to himself, the screaming dynamo took off his shoes and began to stalk around in his stocking feet, yelling, "I order him out of the state of Florida! I'm cleanin' all the clams out of this office!" A clam was an ineffective person. "Out of the state of Florida he goes!"

He rushed out the door, still in his socks, and at the head of the esculator screamed, "Every clam is gonna DIE!"

An aide walked by him and into the office, calmly asking, "What is that madman doing this time?"

Everybody shrugged, went back to work, and in a few minutes, Madman returned for his shoes, laughing. This year, however, the organization had met with initial success—often difficult to adjust to—and there was little madness in the grisly seriousness of 1966.

In the middle of October, one month after he walked out, Don

A Camp Divided 187

Petit returned. He and Bob met to discuss the possibility of Petit's heading up a "Get Out the Vote" campaign. Registered Democrats in Florida exceeded by far the state's registered Republicans, and state Party leaders felt a "Get Out the Vote" campaign was imperative. Petit was open to the idea, and Bob assured him he would be in complete charge; there would be no interference with his authority.

Relations were still amicable between the two, and while they sat around talking, Don offered to call the *Orlando Sentinel*, one of the state's leading conservative newspapers, to see if they had decided upon an endorsement. After a lengthy conversation, he turned to Bob, pleased. The *Sentinel* was going to endorse High. They parted, agreeing to get things moving on the "Vote" campaign.

The next morning Bob went out of town, and someone at headquarters sent a teletype message to all county chairmen.

"Rumors that Don Petit will participate in the campaign are false. There has been no conversation with Mr. Petit. Signed, Robert King High."

Bob was unaware of the lie, and Petit, when he heard, tried unsuccessfully to reach him. Naturally, he thought the teletype went out under Bob's orders.

They got together a couple of days later and resolved the misunderstanding, but the incident was enough to keep Petit from heading the "Vote" drive. It was obvious, he told Bob, that there were individuals who didn't want him around; if he involved himself again, there was no doubt that more frustrations would result, and even more damage to the campaign. Bob nodded; there was logic in that.

Bob went from bleakness to blackness in anxiety over his ego-clashing supporters, but there was less than a month to go now, and with the golden ring so near he didn't have the time or inclination to take sides. So he tried to ignore the conflicts and kept running, sometimes with the current, often against it. For the moment, as Kipling said, the ship was more than the crew.

Bob was in trouble. This was the conclusion he and Baggs reached one day at the *Miami News*, just a few weeks before the election. It was a feeling, an undercurrent of something undefinable, but they agreed the November election strategy was making a candidate out of Republican Claude Kirk.

Bob's strength lay in the large cities, and he was losing ground there. He didn't know it for sure, but he sensed it. As a result, the rural vs. urban pantomime was altered. Kelly and other conservatives were sent into the Panhandle; Bob devoted more time to the cities, hoping it was not too late to recoup.

Reporters found Kirk's "white papers" unrealistic. One called "his promises to make Florida first in about everything without a penny of new taxes" a not-so-funny joke on the voters. But the white papers faded into oblivion when Kirk found a twin-issue to run with, crime and ultra-liberalism. And run he did.

Back in July, Bob and Baggs discussed crime as an issue in the campaign; they felt it should be put in focus, but not in the manner of emotionalism, not a tawdry cry in the night. Then, the Federal Bureau of Investigation released figures showing that the Greater Miami area held the unwelcome distinction of being second in the nation's crime. The FBI figures were a launching pad for the Republican candidate.

Of Bob's administration as Mayor of Miami, Kirk Said, "Under his leadership the city has earned the unenviable reputation of number two crime or sin city in the nation."

Kirk did not say that the Greater Miami area was more than just the City of Miami; it encompassed twenty-six municipalities, including Miami Beach. But who would remember that and who would know it, except for Greater Miami's residents?

In an appeal to fear, Kirk said the city streets were unsafe, particularly for mothers. "In Miami," he told a group in Bonifay, "everyone is locking their doors! " Businessmen in St. Petersburg heard, "I know the Miami market place, and that city has gone down and down. It is a cavity of crime." Political ads on television began to sprout like weeks, and one of the spookiest showed a bedroom enveloped in blackness, a flashlight at the window, a woman's piercing scream. Fear. High was a big, wicked-city mayor, a leader of Babylon.

Bob felt certain Miami voters would not be taken in, and sure enough, Miamians began to resent the way they were being portrayed all over the state. But strange bumper stickers blossomed—"Democrat for Kirk" and "I'm a Demokirk"; Bob, who had been accustomed to taking the offensive, was put in the untenable position of defending. And the worst was yet to come.

Someone said people vote their fears, prejudices, and pocketbooks, in that order. Crime and no new taxes satisfied two of those needs, and it now became prejudice's turn. Bob visited one of the papers in Jacksonville and was informed that, in their judgment, Kirk was ahead. "It's the racial thing," a newsman told him.

In politics the acceptable word for it is ultraliberal, and from north Florida, Kirk said his white papers were no longer an issue in the campaign. Ultraliberalism was the only issue.

He called Bob "a rubber stamp for Washington, backed by the ultraliberals." It was almost funny; Haydon Burns had said High was Bobby Kennedy's man, but now Bob was suddenly the fair-haired boy of LBJ and the Great Society, as Kirk attacked the "ultraliberal philosophies" of High, LBJ, and labor leaders, all in the same breath.

Two reporters who had traveled with Bob were now covering Kirk on the campaign trail. They were at a rally in north Florida and had grown a little sick of hearing the word ultraliberal. Kirk was speaking, leading up to a gambit he had used before, and the reporters decided to have some fun.

"Are there any Republicans in the audience? " Kirk asked. Two or three hands went up.

"Are there any Democrats? " The audience was a mass of raised hands.

"Are there any ULTRALIBERALS? " he shouted. The crowd did not stir. Except for two reporters, who solemnly raised their hands.

Next, the open housing question was injected into the governor's race. In his speeches, the Republican candidate asked, "Do you want open housing?" A political writer stated the obvious. It was an appeal to racism and encouraged a "white backlash" vote.

To make certain no one missed the point and confused ultraliberalism with economy or business policies, the haters went to work again. The state was drenched with the same throwaways, either reprints or leftovers, used during the primaries. One new addition, distributed by the "Committee for Integrity in Government" in Jacksonville and handed out at a Kirk and Leon County GOP booth at a north Florida fair, depicted a cartoon of Bob and the words, "Black power is with you 100 percent, Bob, let's march." Fears, prejudices, and pocketbooks.

Even with Scott Kelly caravaning through the state, the situation for Bob in the Panhandle looked tense. Newsmen were saying that events outside the state, such as the summer race riots and reactions to the war in Viet Nam, were working against the Democratic administration and could have an effect on Florida. They read an anti-Washington vote into Lester Maddox's recent victory in Georgia and wondered if the same thing could happen in the Sunshine State.

CHAPTER FIFTEEN

Then, In a Moment

I had flown but once during the campaign, and then out of necessity, the only way to get back home in time for one of our children's school plays. It was a commercial flight, the weather was bad, and when a hearse pulled alongside the plane and unloaded a coffin, I was sure there would be two bodies aboard before the flight ended. Never again, I vowed.

I was remembering that vow as the private plane in which I sat roared down the runway and up, up into the air.

"Honey," Bob leaned closer, "your nails are digging into my hand."

My nails dug deeper until the "Fasten Seat Belt" light went off. For some reason, when that light goes off, it means everything is all right. It was also the signal for aides and reporters to jump out of their seats and wander around, talking and laughing. I wished they would sit down. They might cause the pilot to lose control of the plane.

A few nights before, Bob had come home with the words, "Faith, you've got to go with me on the plane Thursday."

Couldn't I meet him, I asked? No. There were four cities to cover in one day, a series of rallies, and I had to fly.

"I need you with me, Faith. It's crazy, but I feel like I'll lose if you're not on that plane with me." I went.

Our first landing was in Daytona Beach, where we were met by a caravan of a hundred cars. From there we took to the sky again and headed for Gainesville. Sympathetic aides invited me to play gin rummy. We hit an air pocket and I bid one spade.

"This is High Country" signs still grew in Gainesville, and it was evident there was a thing going between Bob and the college students. He, like most of the young people, was candid, and the lines of communication remained open.

As darkness approached we motorcaded to nearby Starke for a five-county fish fry, complete with mullet and hushpuppies. The sprawling farmer's market was jammed with 5,000 people, and the soft sounds of country music glided on a chilly breeze. Bob and I made our way through the crowd, and it was obvious we were being looked over very carefully. Not a few of the faces held surprise.

Finally, an elderly lady, wiping her hands on an apron, approached me. "I'm so glad to see you, Mrs. High. We all are. I wish you could have heard some o'the things they were sayin' about you up here, and—and, well, now everybody knows it was just vicious gossip! " Her stern, old face softened, she nodded her head and was gone. She had spoken her piece.

Now I understood the earlier expressions of surprise. Most of the faces were warm and friendly, faces of people who worked hard and judged the same way. I was glad I had come.

Back on the plane, we approached Tampa, our last glorious stop. In contrast to my earlier frozen mumblings, I became very talkative.

"Look at the lights of the city! Aren't they gorgeous? Six takeoffs and landings in one day—you know, he's an excellent pilot! Smoothest landing I've ever seen! "

Bob stared at me, then howled with the rest of the group.

The next night in Tampa was a Democratic Party dinner. Head tables were set up on the stage, and Bob and I waited in the wings of the auditorium to enter; we were alone, enjoying music that filtered through the closed curtains.

"You know," Bob said, "I have the feeling that things are picking up again."

The orchestra swung into "I Left My Heart in San Francisco," a favorite of Bob's, and the next thing I knew, we were dancing backstage. As if on cue a policeman entered, followed by aides.

"Just forget about them," Bob whispered in my ear. For once, I did.

Then, in a Moment 193

The last week. After what seemed a lifetime, as if the moment of birth itself opened with the campaign, the trip along the High road was approaching its destination. The week would hold a final journey, one more walkout, and a last-minute assault by outgoing Governor Haydon Burns. It would also usher in a new spirit among High supporters, a sudden camaraderie that refused to be strangled. There would be laughter and tears and a race against time, as Bob crowded a month into seven days.

My final campaign trip began at 4:30 in the morning with five sleepy friends, and by the time we reached the rolling horse country of Ocala, six hours later, we had awakened sufficiently to attend two coffees and watch a statewide telecast of Bob's. Then we headed for the west coast, where we met Bob and his flying entourage, attended more rallies, separated once again, and pointed the car east.

Bob and I were reunited at one o'clock in the morning in Fort Lauderdale, where a proud hotel clerk led us to a "freshly painted Governor's Suite." Though exhausted, Bob walked with a low-keyed buoyancy. All of a sudden, he said, things looked great again. Even reporters had abandoned their pessimism of the month before and looked forward eagerly to the election. Four days away.

"Tired, tired, tired," I sighed, falling into bed.

Half-asleep, Bob mumbled, "Faith, Honey, when are you going to learn to fly?"

I wasn't alone in my plane-phobia, though. Bill Sweisgood was still covering the High campaign for his paper, and on this day's last piece of statewide travel, he was glad the trips in the Galloping Goose would soon be over.

At a barbecue he listened to Bob and a quartet sing, "Just a Closer Walk With Thee." Hm-m-m. That was once. Back on the plane, he had just begun to relax when the pilot turned on some taped music. The first song out? "Just a Closer Walk With Thee." Bill squirmed. That was number two.

A few hours later, returning to the airport for the last flight of the day, the one to Fort Lauderdale, Bill flicked on the car radio.

"And now," said the announcer, "Just a Closer Walk——!"

Number three! Bill had pushed his luck far enough, he decided.

The Galloping Goose could go without him, and dead tired as he was, he rented a car and drove to Fort Lauderdale.

Remembering this latest story Bob had greeted me with, I giggled sleepily. But it was nice to be on the ground, and like Bill must have been doing at that moment, I slept peacefully.

The day before the election, Bob needed a speech and couldn't find his speechwriter. Wilkes, after a dispute with one of the workers, had left.

"Probably gone to the Ocala forest again," an aide said, when Bob tried to locate him.

Wilkes had disappeared several times before, but he always came back, speeches in hand. Bob looked on his moodiness with chagrin, but he tolerated it. This time, however, Wilkes and his speech did not appear.

It was daybreak when Bob called Bill Baggs for help. The speech had to be ready by eleven o'clock, and he could not afford to be late; already, Kirk had reminded crowds his opponent was usually behind schedule in contrast to his own punctuality.

At a recent meeting before realtors in Jacksonville, the two candidates were scheduled to speak at nine in the morning. Herman Terry arrived at Bob's hotel to breakfast with him, and when the candidate had not appeared by 8:30, he got worried. He knew Bob had gone to bed around three and was probably still asleep, and the desk clerk wouldn't give him Bob's room number.

"Only Mr. Wilkes has it. He said he would awaken Mayor High."

Wilkes was still working on the speech, now only fifteen minutes away, and when Herman found Bob by the process of room elimination, it was nine o'clock.

Bob didn't have time to go over his speech, and because he was fifteen minutes late was not allowed to enter the meeting until his opponent finished speaking. Through a crack in the door they heard Kirk's, "and he can't even keep a contract to speak." The audience was hostile, and Bob's stomach had churned over the incident. He didn't want it to happen again.

So Baggs rushed over, and he and Bob began drafting the speech. They had three hours before the eleven o'clock deadline, and at exactly ten they raced downtown to have Baggs' secretary type the speech. Bob made the appointment on time, but Baggs was perturbed. He knew Wilkes would come back eventually, he always did, but he didn't like to see his friend have unnecessary frustrations. There was enough to worry about, like election day and Haydon Burns' sudden attack.

At the eleventh hour, Governor Burns injected himself into the race. Once again he removed the gloves and charged that the Dade County Grand Jury was playing politics by withholding indictments and information detrimental to Bob High, reports which would have a direct bearing on the gubernatorial election.

"My information is that the grand jury has prepared an indictment for a high-ranking officer of the Miami city government, and the judge returned it to be returned to him Tuesday." Tuesday, election day.

It was reminiscent of his previous accusations, for the grand jury foreman replied that there were no unissued indictments. Dade Circuit Judge Henry Balaban called the Governor's accusations a "malicious representation" and challenged him to bring his charges to the grand jury.

Burns answered that other commitments would prevent his appearance in front of the grand jury before Tuesday. "But I will appear later, if there is any point to appearing."

It was almost eerie that the general election campaign was ending on the same note as the primary.

Over the past few weeks, Bob's position in the race had been on the rise again. The slump that developed in midfall seemed to be fading, and the concensus was that the campaign peaked at the right time, close to election day.

A substantial number of the state's political writers foresaw a High victory, even though the margin might be slim.

John McDermott of the *Miami Herald* predicted, "We look for the race to be close. . . . Claude Kirk will make the best showing ever of a Republican candidate for governor . . . but the next governor will be Robert King High."

There were two televised debates between the candidates, and writers generally rated the first one a draw, the second for High. Added to an improved position for Bob were new endorsements: fifteen of Florida's seventeen state attorneys and two former Republican candidates for governor—the first "name" defections from the previously solid Republican party. And for the first time during the governor's race, both hometown dailies endorsed their Mayor, as the *Miami Herald* followed the *News* under the High column.

One worker, still angry over the *Herald*'s lack of support in the primaries, and referring to their record of endorsing losers, said, "Huh! I'm not too sure we ought to have their endorsement. It may be the kiss of death! "

Those willing to trust their crystal balls predicted that 1,200,000 Floridians would go to the polls to elect a governor. Democrats in the state outnumbered Republicans by about four-to-one, and writers wondered how many of those Democrats would abandon ship and vote for the best-financed Republican candidate in the history of Florida?

It was more than a case of Democrats against Republicans. Party lines are of little consideration when a man or woman steps into the voting booth and closes the curtains. Each becomes, not a Republican or Democrat, but an individual guided by mind or emotion, likes or dislikes, love or hate, principle or greed. Few are guided by party, unless it is what that party represents in their own minds.

There had been glaring mistakes in the High campaign, errors of judgment and strategy, personality clashes and problems, but the man himself was what he was, and no amount of mistakes could change that.

The primaries had been like a photograph, sharp, clear, and well-defined. By contrast, the November campaign was more like a double exposure, fuzzy with emotions generated by personalities, words like crime, and ultraliberalism, fear and prejudice—all too obscure to pinpoint. The commodities had been displayed; now it was up to the voter to choose.

Election Eve turned the lights off at our house around midnight, but the darkness did not bring sleep.

"Bob? What do you think? What do you really think? "

There was a silence. I could almost feel his heart pounding underneath the covers, and his voice came out a whisper, as if he were afraid to speak his thoughts aloud.

Then, in a Moment 197

"I think I will be governor tomorrow night."

Then he asked me the question I knew would come, what did I feel? I realized, contrary to my usual flights of intuition, I didn't know. I simply did not feel. Too tired, I supposed. But I wondered why.

Bob tossed and turned. The few hours of sleep left to him would be fitful, merely an ordeal to get through.

I lay awake thinking. It was strange. Bob had been Mayor for over 3,200 days of his life, a fantastic block of time. He had, for a lifetime it seemed, been working toward this night. And in a moment, here it was.

I thought about the significance of a moment. Our chance meeting. Then, in a moment, we were married.

The hopes and ambitions of a boy in Tennessee, the struggles of a young attorney, a salt-and-pepper-haired gentleman who brought the Mayor's chair, a young man from Massachusetts who fed an ideal. Then, in a moment, Bob was running for governor.

The grueling days and nights, the ups and downs, the laughter and the tears. The Issue is Integrity. And now, in a moment, it was over. Only the silence remained.

Tomorrow night around eight o'clock, the votes would begin coming in. Then, in a moment, we would know.

CHAPTER SIXTEEN

The Dream

It was here at last. The time. The moment. The touch of destiny. The elevator creaked to a halt, and Bob and I followed Sargeant Bush through a rear hallway, then a main corridor leading to our hotel suite. As on other election nights the passageway was lined with people and cameras and TV lights, but this was the finale, and everyone became both performer and audience.

A uniformed policeman, standing guard outside our door, looked up from a sheet of paper, smiling. "Just a minute, Mr. Mayor. Can't let you in if your name isn't on the list! "

Bob laughed, casting a sidelong glance at me. I knew what he was thinking. All this fuss, I'll humor her this once. Because of the crush of people in our hotel suite on previous election nights, many of whom we didn't even know, I had plotted with Sargeant Bush to keep the room number secret. We gave it only to our closest friends and certain aides; in turn, the policeman outside the door had a list of names to be admitted. Even Bob did not know the room number in advance.

"You're the most dangerous one of all! " I teased. "At least, if you don't know, you can't be put on the spot! "

A public official should be accessible, but Bob, because of his personality and his usual role of underdog, was sometimes too accessible for his own good.

We entered Suite 304, and friends gathered there swung round to the door. They filled the chairs, perched on beds, leaned against the wall, or paced back and forth in front of the windows. Their

The Dream

too-bright smiles revealed tenseness. My parents had come down from South Carolina and were talking with Mrs. High, fresh from Chattanooga, and Daddy High, just off the campaign trail.

Mrs. High seemed quieter than usual. She might have been thinking back on a conversation with her son nearly a year before when she asked him why he wanted to run for governor. He looked at her silently for a moment, as if trying to crystallize his deepest thoughts, then began talking, almost as if to himself, about the kind of place he wanted his children to grow up in and how few people there were who seemed willing to work toward the future he dreamed of. He ended by looking at his mother quizzically. "If I don't, then who will?"

Bob dashed into the adjoining room to see Bill Poorbaugh and a few aides, while I lingered to talk with friends. At the time, I was struck with the casualness of our conversation, a cover for the feelings underneath; the hour had not yet come when the dam would break. One man, a former neighbor, sat in a chair holding a transistor radio to his ear as if his life depended on it; he seemed oblivious to the presence of others and I had to repeat my question a second time. "What is the count now?"

"Bob's 56,000 behind, statewide." He looked at me in silence, not really seeing me. "But Dade's vote hasn't come in yet." It will, his tone said, it will.

He can't really believe that, I thought. All of a sudden, I knew I didn't. The feeling had been edging its way in since 7:33 that evening, when Bob and I were at home getting dressed, half-listening to the national television network's coverage of around-the-nation elections. The newscaster, a familiar figure on the TV screens of America, was surrounded by electronic computers, playing the favorite game of election night analysts, Projection.

"And now we turn to the state of Florida," the impersonal voice said. Bob glanced at me, his hands stopped in midair in the act of adjusting his tie. "On the basis of our vote analysis, it looks as if an upset is in the making in Florida. We are projecting Republican Kirk over Democrat High in the Governor's race."

Bob paled and uttered something unprintable about computers. For a moment he looked as if he had been stabbed in the back—but only for a moment. He recovered quickly. The computers had done this to him before; he didn't believe it then, and he wasn't going to believe it now.

Funny the things that stick with you. I remembered, not so much the announcer's words, but the hour. For some reason I looked at my watch, like a reflex action. Perhaps I wanted to know the exact moment the dream came crashing down. Seven thirty-three.

Though Bob had been undaunted by the national TV projection, I wondered how he felt in the light of Kirk's 56,000 vote lead. I walked through the connecting door into the next room. Bob was seated on the edge of a bed, talking into the telephone, jotting down figures on a yellow legal pad; Poorboy, hovering over him, looked up.

"It's all right, Faith. Everything's all right."

Bob replaced the receiver and gave me a little one-sided grin. "Hi, Honey." His penetrating look told me he was still trying to believe. "The Dade vote hasn't started to come in yet. It's going to be another one of those! In a minute, we'll go downstairs, just to sort of cheer everybody up."

To cheer everybody up. I walked around to the other side of the bed, behind Bob; he mustn't see my eyes, he could always read them too well. At that moment the hallway door opened, and the policeman admitted two familiar figures, Jenny and Herman. They had just arrived from Jacksonville, and Herman was smiling broadly. Jenny looked frightened as our eyes met. Later she told me that I slowly, almost imperceptibly, shook my head. No one else noticed.

As Bob and I started for the door, he turned to the others. "We'll be back in a few minutes." A pause. "Don't look so glum! You all can give up, but it's not over yet! "

Ernie Bush again led the way to the elevator, through the jammed hallway, past lights, cameras, reporters, and into an overflowing ballroom. One man dashed forward, his face stricken, his hand outstretched.

Bob grasped his hand. "I'm not conceding," he reassured him. "I've been down this road before! "

It was not too difficult to reach the stage, for though the crowd roared with cheers, whistles, and applause, people stepped back, almost automatically, clearing a path for us. Their faces, their eyes, told the reason for their sudden hanging back. The fear. The fear he was going to concede. The hundreds that looked up at the young man standing before the microphone held their breath. Their eyes were afraid and pleading.

"I've come here to see you, to say hello," Bob said. A soft sigh of tremendous relief escaped the crowd, and they broke into renewed cheers. As long as their candidate still believed, they could too; the fear could be pushed back into a dark corner for a while.

"I still believe we can do it," he said. "The Dade precincts will be coming in strong." With a wave of the hand, he was off the stage.

It was not easy to reach the elevator now, for supporters were clutching at happiness again, ready to smile, ready to cheer at anything. A reporter's quick, "Any statement, Mayor?" and Bob's curt, "I just made one," brought responsive applause from those within earshot.

Back in the room Bob returned to working with figures. Kirk's lead of 56,000 was widening, slowly and steadily, and the mood of those gathered in our suite grew quieter, more introspective. While talking with our friends, I found myself watching them, watching all the emotions. It was like viewing a great tide of water run gently down the drain.

"We're not doing what we expected to in Tampa," an aide said.

"That's the story all over," answered Bob. "But I still say, wait for Dade County."

Gene LeBeuf, dropping the telephone, ran his fingers violently through his hair. "Jacksonville, too. They're falling short there, too! What the hell has happened?" He jumped from his chair and began stomping across the room, back and forth, back and forth.

The caller in Jacksonville had told Gene of the horrible gloom in their headquarters. People just sat and stared numbly at the television or glanced, unseeingly, at a sign next to it which said, "Wake up! You can be replaced by a button!"

Jacksonville had paid its own expenses all the way, even helping out the headquarters in Miami occasionally. There, as in other areas of the state, supporters shook their heads, blaming the dwindling votes on the pros.

"Why couldn't they have stayed out of it?" they asked. "This was our campaign! We'd had it since it was a baby." Like a mother, lamenting her dying child.

I was beginning to feel only vaguely present, as the poet who said, "This earth, this time, this life, are stranger than a dream;" yet Bob and Poorboy still hung on. They were the only holdouts, saying, "It could end up as another cliff hanger!"

Poorboy had thought it great when Bob decided to run a second time, and tonight he didn't bother figuring the odds; he didn't need to because he just knew Bob was going to win. Two weeks earlier they had discussed a poll which showed Bob losing by two or three percent. "What do you think?" Bob asked.

"You'll win," Bill stated flatly.

Bob was concerned over Kirk's promises of no new taxes. "I'm afraid he's getting through to the people."

"No!"

"But it's what they want to hear." And he was concerned about the power structure in Florida; politicians usually went with the power structure, the big businesses. Bob had leveled with them, letting them know he believed in big business paying its share of taxes. After he won the nomination, an official from one of the phosphate industries joked with him on the matter of taxes.

"You weren't really serious about that, were you, Mayor?"

"Yes, I was."

And now the last shred of hope. Dade's vote was finally coming in, only it was not the huge majority Bob had counted on. It was too little and too late.

Bob's face was a mask, but his tightly clenched jaw and the fixed look in his eyes told of a man fighting against shock. The Magic City had turned fickle this night. She was only teasing him before.

The telephone rang again, and I answered. It was Baggs, and somehow, I had to hear it from him. "It's all over, isn't it, Bill?" I whispered.

A fraction of a second slipped by. "I'm afraid so."

I handed the receiver to Bob and walked over to the window to take my turn at staring at the blackness. The Magic City twinkled and sparkled as never before, and I thought, you're a traitor. No, that wasn't right.... I glanced around at Bob and the pain was beginning to show in his eyes.

"Well, Don...," Bob looked at Wilkes, who had entered the room earlier. "I guess this is it. We may as well start drafting the concession speech."

There might well have been a soft thud in the room, for that was the effect of Bob's words. There was a pitiful silence, broken only by the gliding of feet across the carpet as, one by one, men filed into the next room or out in the hall to await the drafting of the speech.

One of the last to leave the room was Daddy High. Bob walked up to him and put his arm around his shoulder; the elderly man looked down at the floor for a moment, then up at his son. It was a time when two men are unashamed to cry. The next morning would reveal a similar incident at our home, when Bob put his arm around our son and said, "I'm sorry, Bobby. We didn't make it."

Bob and Wilkes began writing the concession speech, and I joined our friends in the next room. It was like a death watch. The world would go on, of course, and if the ideals were worthwhile, they would pick themselves up, brush off the dust and start again, even if it meant starting at the beginning. But a beginning had been made, and Florida politics would never be quite the same again.

Word spread rapidly into the hall, then the ballroom, that Bob was conceding. Word came back that a few persons were leaving, not waiting to hear the concession, but most were staying, rooted to the spot. It was another unique feature of the campaign, for whoever heard of sticking by a losing candidate?

The connecting door between the rooms opened and Gene motioned me over. The speech was finished, he said, and Bob wanted me to hear it before we went downstairs. The others began leaving to go to the ballroom, and I joined the handful in the next room: Bob, Poorboy, Wilkes, and Gene.

"We've finished it, Honey," Bob said. "Tell us what you think." He was composed, but the pain and shock showed through as do the pebbles at the bottom of a clear stream. And some way, somehow, he would have to bear his pain alone; no one else could take it for him.

Bob began in a clear, firm voice, breaking the stillness of a room that seemed to hold its breath with words from the secret soul of a man. Poorboy, Gene, Wilkes, and I must have mirrored each other's emotions, staring hard at Bob's face, blinking rapidly to keep the brightness inside our eyes. And Bob continued reading.

"I was born the son of a Tennessee carpenter-farmer." There was a slight skip in his voice. "I became the Democratic candidate for Governor of this great state. Such an opportunity could have happened only in America." He could not go on.

"Bob, please...," I began. It was sheer torture for him. "Give another speech, a shorter one or something."

He shook his head, regaining control, and started over again. Gene's face was darkened and contorted, and he jumped from his chair and left the room, tears streaming down his cheeks; Wilkes sat staring at the floor; Poorboy flicked wet eyes back and forth between Bob and the window, murmuring, "I don't believe it. I just don't believe it."

Bob got through the entire speech and lifted vulnerable eyes to me. "Well?"

"It's beautiful." I was choking. The speech was more than pretty words on a piece of paper; the speech was Bob High, the man, and he was right. It was a speech he had to give.

It was time to go, time to face the people and the cameras, time to take the last walk up the High road, time to reach the peak. We walked out into the hallway, still lined with people and cameras and television lights, and two supporters, a man and wife, walked over to us.

"Bob, Faith," the man was crying. "A bunch of us wanted to give you all something. We . . . we hoped you could take these to Tallahassee . . . ," and his voice crumbled. He thrust a long, black box at Bob, and his wife handed me a similar one. The hallway grew hushed, heads pushed closer to see.

The boxes held two gold watches. Inscribed on Bob's was, "Governor Robert King High," and on mine, "Florida's First Lady."

We continued the long walk down the hall to the elevator, again following Sargeant Bush, again squeezing between people and cameras, clinging to each other's hands. The elevator wobbled

The Dream

down two floors, came to a halt, and we stepped into the ballroom. Faces and figures stood out in sharp relief against a haze of smoke that floated in the air, and when the crowd spotted Bob they burst into a delirium of cheers and shrieks and weeping, the only way they had to let him know he was still their candidate.

The band began playing, "Hey, Look Me Over," and as on the night of the runoff, everyone wanted to shake hands with Bob, to touch him. But for different reasons than before; they wanted to share his disappointment, to let him know they felt the pain, too.

Of all the reactions, the ones that stabbed me the most were those of the reporters, the busy breed of men called cynical and worldly wise. They wrote fast—they had to, to catch their precious color—but they were writing while jaw muscles twitched, while biting a lip, while tears streamed down their faces. One of the long-time members of the Rumpled Retinue could not write, and as we passed by him, he threw his note pad to the floor and turned his face to the wall. I wondered how many had mistaken cynicism of the press for a protective covering around the heart.

At last we were onstage, and as one reporter said, the hundred-odd paces from elevator to stage was the longest walk of Bob High's life. As he stood before them in front of the microphones, the frenzied cries began again. Bob's face had lost its color, but he was still smiling at the hundreds who cheered him, hundreds who had not gone home. Under ordinary circumstances, a loser's headquarters would be almost deserted. But these were no ordinary circumstances. Those supporters, regardless of their differences, had a quality the candidate himself had, and demanded. Loyalty. Even the ones who had a particular ax to grind must have recognized something, that Integrity was not just a word, after all.

The cheers died down. A quiet settled over the ballroom. I saw the sudden clenched jaws, heard the sharply drawn breaths, felt the quick tenseness of the crowd as the dreaded moment arrived. I looked at Bob, breathed a silent, please let him get through it, and took a deep breath.

The cameras angled in, and Bob, smiling grimly, began to speak in clear, measured tones. "I lost this election—but I say to my fellow Floridians that defeat is swallowed up in victory.

"I was born the son of a Tennessee carpenter-farmer. I became the Democratic candidate for Governor of this great state. Such an opportunity for honor and service—for a farm boy born in poverty—could have happened only in America." The eyes that looked up at him from the ballroom were bright and reddened, and from somewhere came a muffled sob.

"I must be worthy of such an honor and such a heritage. I can be worthy only if I accept this election's result in a spirit of grace, just as I would have welcomed victory in a spirit of joy.

"I say, 'the people give and the people take away. Blessed be the name of the people.

"I thank my fellow Democrats for the nomination they gave me. I thank my fellow Floridians for the kindness they showed me. I thank all those who worked in my campaign for their labor, their loyalty, and their love.

"I wish Mr. Kirk Godspeed and all good success as Governor. He will be my governor.

"I am a Floridian. I love my state more than I care for my political fortunes. I will be a good citizen. I will be faithful and dutiful."

Reporters' pencils were flying; their expressions showed even they had not expected a speech such as this.

"Prominent in my thoughts tonight are the young people," Bob continued. "They must interest themselves in the new politics we were trying to build in Florida.

"I ask all Floridians to join me in doing all we can to make the next four years good years for Florida."

He paused and looked into the faces of the assembled throng, faces that wept quietly. His expression, a kind of eloquent sadness, told them the curtain was falling.

"Now, my fellow Floridians, I have these last words.

"I may have tears in my eyes—but I have gratitude in my heart.

"I thank you."

A sound that was almost a wail broke from hundreds of throats. Bob turned to me and kissed me, and I thought, I should have known he could get through it. He wasn't completely alone, after all, for God had given him what he needed to get through the long night.

One thing was indisputable. It was about the seed, the seed that was born a long time before, that was watered and took root. Tonight that seed had blossomed.

For days after the election the newspapers speculated on why Bob lost, why Kirk won, why people vote the way they do. According to the analysts, many diversities went into the election of Florida's first Republican governor in nearly one hundred years. An anti-Washington vote. White backlash. Scott Kelly. Haydon Burns. Faulty strategy.

Florida was not the only state swept by the Republican tide; it washed over most of the nation. Dissatisfied with the war in Viet Nam, racial troubles, and the Great Society, Floridians could do something about their frustrations. They could vote against Democrat High. Bob, because he was a Democrat, became identified with the "ins"—and 1966 was not a year for the in-crowd. It was ironic because he had always been associated with what the papers called "the little people," against the power structure and the sacred cows.

Writers linked faulty campaign strategy with Scott Kelly and the rural-urban question. Candidate High had spent too much time in small counties, feeling secure in the urban areas of the state, and when it came time to vote, even the big cities turned their backs on him.

After the defeat, Don Petit said, "Scott Kelly has succeeded in doing in seven weeks what the Republican party has been trying to do for ninety-four years. He led my candidate to ruins."

Kelly was onstage during Bob's concession speech, and afterwards, when Bob introduced him to the audience, there was only polite applause, sprinkled with a few boos. But Bob introduced him as "the State Senator . . . my friend," and they clasped shoulders, man-fashion. It was an emotional moment for the two, and Bob was still unwilling to write Kelly off.

The other name most frequently mentioned in assessing Bob's loss was Haydon Burns. As far as Bob was concerned, the name Burns spelled traitor, but he said, "I don't hate Haydon. He reacts one way, I react another."

Perhaps the word react was the major piece in the jigsaw puzzle of politics. Writers who grouped ultraliberalism, crime, and taxes may have hit closer to the truth than anyone else, for the voter, when he steps into the booth and closes the curtains, is doing more than just voting. He is reacting.

Weeks later, Bob spoke of voters themselves not knowing what moves them to vote as they do. "Frustrations, anxieties, bewilderments, build up a deposit of general rage and impatience against things as they are."

Of the hate and the hate literature inspired by the word ultra-liberalism, Bob seemed baffled. "I had no idea of the magnitude of it."

So the voter listens, but often he doesn't hear. He reacts with emotion, fears and prejudices, loves and hates. Such a simple thing—and so complex.

Florida politicians mumbled quietly, more convinced than ever before that "you can't win without the power structure." But politicians do not always learn their lessons, for though Bob wanted desperately to be governor, he wanted to be governor for all: the power structure, the little man, black or white, farm or city. No longer was it true that in Florida, big money captured the Democratic nomination, and in the Sunshine State the face of politics, Bob-High-fashion, was signalling a change. He wanted a clean win or no win at all, so maybe, he said, he paved the way for someone else.

As a *Miami News* editorial put it, "Mr. High tried very hard to create a new mood in Florida politics. He did not duck a single one of those issues that most Southern politicians have been ducking for years.

"Our hope is that in losing, he prepared the ground for a host of young men who might now get into politics with the noble ideas that made Mr. High's candidacy so attractive."

The final figures in the governor's race were High, 668,233, and Kirk, 821,190, figures that were to keep Bob awake for many and many a night. On our way out of town a few days after the election, he was recognized by a woman in a Jacksonville coffee shop.

"I didn't vote for you. I voted for Kirk." She paused. "I heard your concession speech. I think I made a mistake."

The woman was not alone in her reaction. Bob's concession

The Dream

speech seemed to give Floridians a picture of himself that he was never able to get across during the campaign.

A philosopher once said, "Someday the world will break your heart." For a little while, it broke Bob's. He did not sleep at all the night of the election; I awoke several times during the night to find him up at the window, staring out, or walking back and forth across the floor. He had once said, "I can't put into words how much I want to be governor." Seeing his dejected figure in the darkness, alone with his thoughts and heartbreak, I didn't need to hear him put anything into words.

For the next few days Bob was a man in deep shock. Once, while watching our children playing on the lawn, he said, "It's an agonizing irony."

"What is?"

"The crime thing. For years I've taken a stand against crime, but the crime issue was used against me." And he sighed, "Oh, well...."

What seemed to hurt him the most was his belief that people never really understood him. "They never understood—they never understood what I meant by Jeffersonian democracy is that government lives and moves and has its being in the will and consent of the people." In a campaign speech, Bob had said, "Thomas Jefferson was the greatest of all Americans. That is one reason I am a Democrat. The Democratic Party is the party that Jefferson built."

I remembered our visit to Monticello, the dreams of Jefferson that had somehow become the dreams of Bob High. A better place is what it all boiled down to. It was like Eldorado, the fabled city of gold that the Spanish conquerers searched for in vain; it came to mean a hope or a dream worth a lifetime's search—even if that hope was never fulfilled. Such was the Florida Governor's race of 1966. It was Bob High's Eldorado.

The road back was a long one, for you don't forget a lifetime overnight. At his first City Commission meeting after the election, supporters jammed the chambers sporting "It's High Time!" buttons. They had not forgotten either.

A reporter asked Bob if he would ever run for election again. He thought a minute. "I am a public man. If there is opportunity and hope, I won't shrink from it."

In December the City began to attack excessive automobile insurance rates, and two months later Miami investigated the County's tax assessing practices. Bob was back in the fray, saying, "The large businesses and corporations are not paying their fair share. This puts a 100 percent burden on the homeowner and small business man."

He threw himself into the winter and spring months, trying to catch up on a huge backlog of law cases, trying to raise funds to pay off a campaign deficit, trying to forget. There were still nights when he awakened in a cold sweat, after dreaming he had won the governor's race.

"You know, Faith," he said, "sometimes I wake up and my stomach feels like it's tied in knots."

Early summer came, and still Bob blamed himself. He blew it, he said, there was something more he could have done. And besides, he had really wanted to do something for the people. And the people didn't like him.

Slowly, slowly, he began to agree with friends who kept telling him the vote was not a personal thing, that it was just a crazy mixture of the times and of chance, and the old High spirit, submerged deep inside for the past few months, began digging its way out.

By mid-August, after our trip to Canada's Expo '67, Bob looked better than he had in months. Our children were overjoyed at having their daddy full time again, and the feeling was mutual; the front yard football games resumed, and two of the girls fell next in line for trips to Nicaragua and Hawaii. Bob's jovial, boyish smile flashed often, and he was beginning to know what it was to be happy again.

He joked with Poorboy one day, discussing the new Republican Governor's problems, and Bill asked him what he thought about running again in 1970.

"You've gotta be kidding! " he laughed. "But I'll tell you what. If things in Tallahassee are as bad then as they are now, I'll just say, 'Claude, you've made a hell of a mess! Move over! ' " He was himself at last.

The Dream

In 1964 Bob addressed a group of young people on "What It Takes to Make a Man Great." Now, almost three years later, and three years wiser and stronger, his words took on added significance.

"Greatness is," he had said, "to believe in and to practice those standards which represent the highest moral quality of mankind, and to reflect them with such strength and conviction that other men are moved to follow them.

"A firm belief in God is the bedrock foundation of greatness, with the tempering of all our acts on the mighty anvil of His Son, Jesus Christ.

"The second standard of greatness is purpose. A great man may be defeated—momentarily, discouraged—occasionally. But he will pursue a steadfast course in the face of any and every obstacle.

"A man must be an explorer, a pioneer—for himself, and for other men.

"A great man must be a student. He must study his time and his people.

"To be great he must have compassion.

"The sixth layer is leadership, but that is not enough; Adolph Hitler was a leader, and so is Fidel Castro. For without the bedrock foundation, without purpose and compassion, no leader can be great."

There were some who might have said Bob High defined himself in that speech. Certainly God had given him the opportunity to practice greatness, and he knew there were still opportunities and hopes and ideals. If you believe in them, you don't ever give up.

CHAPTER SEVENTEEN

The Dream That Would Not Die

August 30, 1967. The night was clear and cloudless; the air hung heavy with late summer heat. Once again, as on a November night which seemed a thousand years ago, the moon was shining down on Bayshore Drive, casting a diffused spotlight on the white-columned home.

Every window was ablaze, but this time there was a subtle difference. The house no longer stood in jewel-like brilliance, as it had in November; the glow had faded to a flat, white pallor. The French windows on the first floor seemed to stare sightlessly into the dark night; most of the second floor windows were partially covered with shades, like lidded eyes afraid to look at what was held inside.

Cars crowded the long driveway and spilled over on the lawn. This time, however, reporters from the papers and the radio and TV stations had parked along the street, outside the closed wooden gate. They moved aimlessly about or stood talking in small groups; some were writing into notebooks, one man stopping to brush at something that blurred his eyes. Cameras dangled limp from shoulders; now and then, a new arrival joined the two uniformed policemen who stood sentry at the gate.

On the bricked porch, cigarettes glowed like fireflies. The small cluster of persons there was not saying much, just staring into the darkness.

A taxi pulled up and one of the policemen peered inside, then motioned to his companion to open the gate. Two people

The Dream That Would Not Die

emerged, a man and a woman, each carrying a suitcase. For them, as for all the others, it had begun that afternoon. . . .

Herman Terry was driving up Peachtree Street. He had just dropped Jenny off at Lenox Square to do some shopping and was on his way to keep a business appointment. Day-old fugitives from the heat of Jacksonville, they couldn't wait to get on to the cool mountains around Hendersonville. A few days up there might ease some of the weariness that still hung on, even after nine months, from Bob's campaign. He shook his head, remembering the long days and bitter disappointment.

It was just before three o'clock, and the afternoon sun glowed like an oven. Good grief, Atlanta's traffic was worse than Jacksonville's. His thoughts returned to his friend. It was a shame he and Jenny couldn't have gotten reservations to go to Expo '67 with Bob and Faith. They would have had a good time together; they always did. Maybe they could plan a trip to New England in the fall. Jenny and Faith had been wanting to get at those antiques for two years now! On the phone last week, Bob suggested, a little wistfully, that he come to Miami for a visit. He wanted to go, but he just couldn't get away.

Herman had the car radio on, enjoying the music as it drifted in and out of his thoughts. The haunting violin suddenly broke off in the middle of a note. The sound of a teletype cut in, signaling a news bulletin.

"We interrupt this program to bring you a special bulletin: at 2:35 this afternoon, Mayor Robert King High of Miami died in a Coral Gables hospital. We repeat, at 2:35 this afternoon, Mayor Robert King High of Miami died in a Coral Gables hospital."

My God! He had to find Jenny, get a plane to Miami. Oblivious to honking horns, he made a quick U-turn in the middle of the street. Herman knew the expressway would be faster back to Lenox Square, but he didn't know how to find it, so he fought the traffic and the red lights, trying to hear—and trying not to hear—the professional voice of the newscaster that kept cutting back in with the terrible bulletin.

Lenox Square was a maze of shops, and he had no idea which one Jenny was in. He'd try Davidson's first. He went directly to her.

Jenny looked up in surprise. Then she noticed the awful set of his face. "Herm, what's wrong?"

"Come on. I'll get the car."

"Oh! Something has happened," she said to the elderly woman who was waiting on her.

At the car Herman looked as if his face were about to explode. Still he said nothing. He went around to his side and got in. Jenny looked at him, waiting for the answer. Later she remembered that his jaw muscle was beginning to work strangely. He cleared his throat.

"Bob. . .," he said. "Bob died."

It was the first time she had ever seen him cry.

The law offices of High, Stack, and Davis were as busy as usual. Joan Robinson, the receptionist, had done nothing all day but answer phones, yet she wasn't complaining. Things had worked out so beautifully for her.

Only three weeks ago she moved back to Miami from the west coast of Florida. She had needed an apartment and a job and had walked into both. The Highs were personal friends, and how fortunate the Mayor's receptionist had gotten married, leaving this spot for her.

Another call. Joan looked indignant. "No! Of course that's not true! " Replacing the receiver, she glanced up at Miss Moyer, who had paused by the desk at the tone in Joan's voice. Miss Moyer's eyes were question marks.

"Some people surely have nerve! Do you know what that man said? He said he'd heard the Mayor had had a heart attack and wanted to know if it was true! What an awful rumor."

Another light on the switchboard flashed, and after a brief exchange, she turned back to Miss Moyer. "My Lord! That was someone who said they heard he had died! "

Suddenly all the lights on the board began flashing. Within minutes, every secretary in the office was needed to answer the calls and issue denials to the same questions. Miss Moyer was ready to cry. The city had gone insane!

Over the rising din, Joan's voice sounded shrill. "No sir, it is not true. Mayor High is out of the city. It is a terrible, terrible rumor."

The secretaries believed their boss was out of town because that

The Dream That Would Not Die

was what they were told. Early that morning, one of his last instructions had been, "Faith, don't let anyone know where I am. Call the office and say I'm out of town." He did not want the public to know his heart might be acting up again.

Now Joan glanced up from the switchboard and saw that the reception room had filled with people. The place was a madhouse! Well, she had to stay with the telephones right now. The person peering in through the glass looked like a reporter from the *Miami News*.

"Tell the Judge it is not true," she said into the phone. The reporter walked into her office and was now standing at her side, looking down at her in a funny sort of way. She turned back to the telephone.

"Please listen." The secretary on the other end of the line was crying. "It just isn't true. Tell the Judge the Mayor is out of town. Someone has started a terrible rumor, I don't know why they would do that to him, and—wait a minute."

The reporter gently touched Joan on the arm. Tears coursed down his rough cheeks. "Honey, it *is* true."

Bud Stack and his wife, Barbara, were in New York. He had placed a call to his brother, Bob Lazenby, in Miami, asking him to see about a small matter, saying yes, they'd had a great time in Canada and would be home in a couple of days. Bud and Barbara went out for lunch, then returned to their hotel. The red message light on the telephone was flashing.

"A Mr. Lazenby in Miami has called twenty or thirty times," the operator said.

In a moment Bob Lazenby was on the line. "Bud? I don't know how to tell you this." Silence. "I don't know how to tell you this." Another silence. "Bob High is dead."

"What? What did you say?"

"Bob is dead."

"What happened? What do you mean?"

"He had a heart attack."

"No, no, no!"

Moments later, his wife called out from the dressing room. "Bud? Do you hear someone groaning?"

When he did not answer, she peered around the corner. The groans were coming from her husband.

They caught a plane for Miami, and because they didn't have time to pack, they stowed presents for their children beneath the seat; Bud had to hold a child-sized teddy bear on his lap.

My God, he thought, how opposite everything seems. Our hearts take a beating, and yet we look like drunks poised between parties. My God, my God.

He remembered meeting Bob and later joining the law firm. And he remembered the last time he had seen him. They were walking from the office to the parking lot. At the corner, Bob suddenly stopped.

"I've got to quit smoking these cigars! They're going to ruin me. I can hardly catch my breath! "

They climbed into the car, discussing Bud's vacation, and Bob told him to "really enjoy" himself. "Let your hair down and relax! "

"That's a twist! You usually push for more work! " He hadn't seen Bob looking so good or seeming so happy in ages, certainly not since the campaign.

The cigars came up again, and Bud said, "Why don't you quit? I'll bet you $50 you can't stop smoking those damn things. I'll even make it a hundred! "

"Let's start the bet after Saturday. I want to smoke one at the Pro game! "

"No bet! "

"Well . . . call me tomorrow and I'll see."

Bud had called, but the subject of cigars did not come up. Now it never would. And here I sit with this damn teddy bear. My God, my God.

I looked at our house as if I were suddenly seeing it as a person, an old retainer, almost a member of the clan. Suffering as the rest of us suffered. The big white home was ill-prepared for the shock and even less so for the onslaught of those bearing their grief, carrying it like a piece of unwanted luggage.

The house was built by Jack Peacock, the "father of Coconut Grove," in 1909, but it had worn its years with dignity and grace and pride until, on this sultry afternoon in August, its age caught up with it, making it look old and tired and frightened.

It suddenly was faced with the unbearable truth that the vibrant gentleman who had looked at it with such pride would look no more. Its walls would no longer echo with his deep voice as it rollicked through "Up a Lazy River"; they would have to be content with the hollow notes of a memory. The Click! Click! Slap! of the billiard balls and the challenging laughter of father and son must be tucked away in the heart of the old house; and on some future night, when it could bear to pull the memories out, it would remember, and smile.

Even as it sunk deeper and deeper into shock, old and tired as it had become, it had the breeding to know that it must summon up what little courage was left and allow its doors to be opened to those who suffered with it.

I didn't wait for the ringing of the bell. I had seen the approaching figures through the French windows and went to meet them.

Scott Kelly and Gene LeBeuf walked in, a little hesitantly. They had not expected to see me at the door and didn't quite know what to say to a woman who had been a widow for only a couple of hours.

"Faith, I . . . I just heard." Scott's face matched his grey suit.

"Did you just fly in, Scott?"

"No, I was here, got in around noon. I was going to call Bob. I . . . God!"

Gene was standing inside the doorway, quiet, fists clenched at his sides, mouth in a firm line. He looked as if he were holding his breath.

"Gene." I held out my hands to him, and he grabbed them, opened his mouth to speak. But no sound came out. His eyes rested on me for a moment, then darted away; his handsome face started to crack, his hand shot up to his eyes as it had on a November night a thousand years ago, and he walked like a blind man into the dining room.

Once the news was out, friends had begun coming, filling the dining room, the living room, the kitchen. A few of the men walked back and forth outside, kicking at the grass; some were grouped around the pool table, just standing there, staring at the empty pockets. All, in their common grief and shock, were drawn to the one place there was for them to go. Bob's home.

They didn't need to talk to one another. They walked around, sat and stared into space, drifted into the kitchen for the endless cups of coffee, listened to the news reports on TV, still not believing it, looked up at each ring of the doorbell to see who the new arrival was, avoided looking at that picture of Bob in the Florida room—the thoughtful pose used so much in the campaign—or looked at it, uncomprehendingly, and walked around some more. Anyway, they were there, and they knew instinctively how Bob would have felt: he would have wanted them, expected them, to be there. Whatever characteristics they had, individually or as a group, they had the loyalty Bob had valued. And they would be loyal to the bitter end.

Mr. and Mrs. High arrived quite late, pale and tired. Mrs. High retired, but Daddy High chatted fondly with friends. He reminded them of happy days, days when the hot, dusty roads of north Florida were cooled with an icy Coke and tales on the courthouse steps about a young man who was running for governor, a boy who wasn't a big-time city slicker as they'd been led to believe, even though he was the Mayor of Miami, but knew what it was to feel the good earth under his toes, the melting sun of the country on his back. The spring of the hills was gone from Daddy High's step this night. But he still had that indomitable spirit which made him hold his head high, allowed him to remember, and to talk with his son's friends of the things he remembered. He was a symbol for them, and they clung to that symbol gratefully.

At least it had happened the way Bob would have wanted it to, in the thick of a battle. Governor Kirk and the teachers of Florida had long been at odds, and the prospect was bright for the closing of public schools in Florida. This was too much for Bob to ignore.

Less than twenty-four hours before his death, he fired off telegrams to the President of the Florida Senate and the Speaker of the House, urging them to seek a special session of the legislature to meet the needs of education. Believing that the school crisis which threatened Florida's children overrode party affiliation, he ended the wire with these words:

"This is no time to be Republicans or Democrats—but Floridians." It was the last missive which would be signed, Robert King High, Mayor of Miami.

Epilogue

America wears many faces.

With the 1980's breathing down her neck, lines from Macbeth echo hauntingly toward the twentieth century. "I think our country sinks beneath the yoke; it weeps, it bleeds, and each new day a gash is added to her wounds." This is the tormented face of America.

Yet there is another face.

It is embodied in a passage from Thomas Wolfe, one Bob used so often that many of us came to know it by heart. "To every man his chance—to every man his shining, golden opportunity—to every man the right to live, to work, to be himself, and to become whatever his manhood and his vision can combine to make him. This is the promise of America."

The dissenters scoff, we've seen her promises, but where the hell is she going? We've got black power, flower power, you-name-it power, but have we got a destiny?

Bob had his own answer.

"We must all," he said, "rich and poor, young and old, black and white, decide what our national destiny is and work toward that end.

"America is going through a spiritual crisis. The outcome amounts to a historical turnabout. Decent politics. And decent politics means decent politicians.

"The politician, as we have known him, is in the sunset of his existence.

Epilogue 221

"This imposes on us, and on my younger friends especially, the obligation to do better than you have done, and to be a participant and not merely a witness in this change."

What is a man, if his chief good and market of his time be but to sleep and feed? A beast, no more. This was the new mood Bob was forever talking about.

There are many roads, and Bob's happened to be politics. His was no lily-livered existence. It was touched by pride and ego, for he was, after all, only a man. Yet in going back over the pieces of his life, one thing stood above all others. It was compassion for his fellow man.

A few weeks before his death, he spoke of compassion without calling it by name. He was taping a radio program, and there was no script, just off-the-cuff ramblings. The moderator asked him how he would define success.

"Success is dependent on your belief in your fellow man," Bob said. "It can't be a goal all by itself. If so, then it becomes the paramount objective, shallow and superficial."

He talked about a public official being a trustee for the people—for the millions of dollars of their tax monies. And to be trusted by the people was a mark of success.

"There is always a place for a man who believes in the people and is willing to fight for their cause," he said.

"In big cities, in life, it's hard to find someone who will listen, someone to turn to for help. People rush around with no time or concern for someone else's problems. As Mayor, I can do things the average person feels ought to be done but has no voice to do them with.

"People can become so discouraged, despondent, demoralized. Sometimes one needs to be told," and his voice carried the weight of experience, "that one, two, or three defeats is not the end.

"No one can do anything by himself—you need people. And a person is a very valuable and wonderful thing.

"To be able to help your fellow man is what life is all about." And the reason, perhaps, he made an issue out of integrity.

He mulled over the words from Ecclesiastes, "a time to love and a time to hate," and he said the hour had come to stop hating. "If I were a minister, I would do what I could to eradicate hate. It is something this country can do without and one of the great wastes of human personality.

"Since the beginning—since Christ—there has been hate. His life points out what man's hate can do."

Bob's final words on that tape echo even now, across the waves of rioting and discontent. "It may be difficult to love your fellow man, but—stop hating."

Months after he died someone asked a couple of High supporters what they thought of the Governor. "Our governor is dead," they replied.

And after the campaign, Poet Laureate Bill dropped his joking and grew serious. He spoke of his association with Bob and the campaign.

"It made me feel clean." The five words said more than a thousand.

Though deeply involved, Bob traveled much of his road alone. To him it was the best of two worlds: needing people to love and be loved by, while being alone with his thoughts, his dreams, and his Creator. This was how Bob High came to believe, how he came to care.

Eleven days after losing the governor's race, Bob spoke to the newspaper editors and publishers of Florida. It was his first public address since losing the election. A difficult speech for him to make. He said if he were to do it over again, he would repeat the same things. He would change nothing.

He concluded, "I hope that after I am gone there will be someone who can say, his life had a snatch of honor in it."

After his death, I found a folded magazine page in one of his suit pockets. The page looked a hundred years old. For nine months he had unfolded and refolded it, because of the message it carried:

"Far better it is to dare mighty things, to win glorious triumphs, even though checkered with failure, than to take rank with those poor spirits who neither enjoy much nor suffer much, because they live in the grey twilight that knows not victory nor defeat."

Politics under the sun may never be the same after the romantic adventure that began on the High road. Bob learned what politics was, that it was more than a means to an end. Rather it was a means to accomplish certain things, to make things better. Politics as usual and the usual politicians were on the way out.